Life and Loss

Legacy Writing

IN THE AGE OF COVID—19

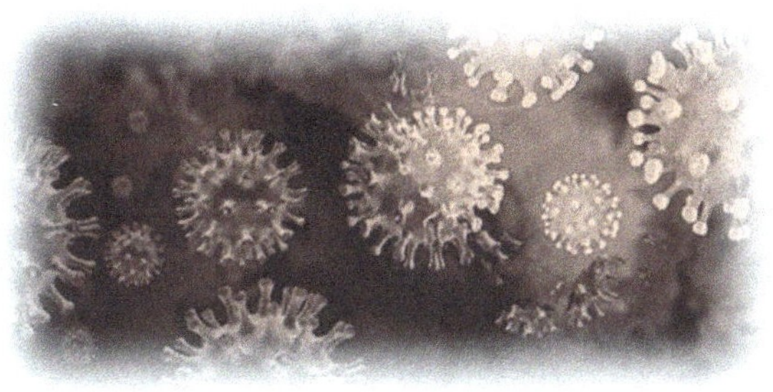

Rachael Freed

Life and Loss: Legacy Writing in the Age ofCOVID-19
©Rachael Freed

Cover Design: © Gigi Stillman
Interpretation: Devastation–COVID–19 ©Isaac Joseph Julson
Interior Design: AI Assistant, Chat GBT in collaboration with the ©author

For reprint permissions, or for information about quantity discounts for educational or fundraising purposes by organizations and institutions, contact MinervaPress1@gmail.com

For information or to explore legacy writing resources, visit www.Life-Legacies.com or email the author at rachaelfreed@icloud.com

ISBN:

Hardcover Edition ISBN 979-8-234-07545-1
Softcover Edition ISBN 978-0-9817450-4-6
E-book Edition ISBN 978-0-9817450-9-1

Printed and Bound by Lightning Source in the United States of America

First Edition, 2026 MinervaPress

Covid–Devastation

Author's Note

This book was born in a time of great silence and greater change. I did not write it to explain the global COVID-19 pandemic, but to remember its significance and consequences to the twenty-first century.

These pages carry not only my voice but the voices of many friends, colleagues, healers, poets, and legacy writers whose reflections on loss, grief, resilience, and transformation shaped my work. Their reflections, poems, and legacy letters have been included with minute editorial changes and reproduced with permission from the original authors.

I offer this not as a definitive history but as a bridge … from memory to meaning, from grief to blessing, from one generation to the next. And to remember the significance and consequences of Covid–19 for those of us who lived it in the twenty–first century.

- Rachael Freed

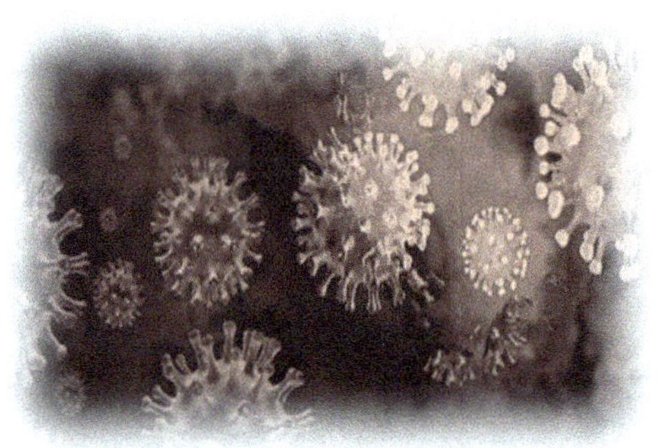

"Losing too is still ours; and even forgetting

still has a shape in the kingdom of transformation.

When something's let go of, it circles; and though we are rarely the center of the circle it

draws around us its unbroken, marvelous curve."

– Rainer Maria Rilke

Dedication

This book is for continuity and for the future.

I dedicate it

To my grandparents and parents

and as a legacy

for our planet's grandchildren and theirs,

and especially for mine, with my love:

Sophie Bea	*Mitch*
Sam	*Lily*
Isaac	*Harry*
Aidan	*& Gigi*

Contents

Preface

By Teresa Schreiber Werth

Editor of *Navigating the Pandemic; Stories of Hope and Resilience*

At 77, I have lived through some pretty memorable moments in history: the moon landing, the Viet Nam War, the assassination of JFK, Martin Luther King, Robert Kennedy and George Floyd, Watergate, 9/11, the Challenger explosion, the first Trump era, Columbine, COVID... just a very small list of the significant events that have happened in my lifetime. These are events I can talk about and about which I remember many details. My children and grandchildren seldom ask me about any of these events and I don't make a point of sharing these memories.

Until Rachael prompted my thinking about my personal history when I took a class from her about writing Legacy Letters many years ago, I never gave these types of experiences much thought. It never occurred to me that each of these, and so many more, influenced my life, my perception of the world and shaped my values, priorities and beliefs.

With this enlightenment about passing on our personal values, beliefs and experiences, I realized all of the opportunities I have missed to ask my parents and grandparents so many questions about their lives. I most deeply regret the questions I never asked my own parents. Aside from some cold, hard genealogy research, the chances are long gone to learn about their lives, to ask questions, to listen to their stories or to be guided by their values.

Energized by a new understanding of the importance of passing on our unique stories, I began by making a list of the topics about which I want to write letters for my three grandchildren. That list is a living, breathing document that continues to grow. It now includes topics related to COVID-19, our pandemic.

If you haven't been inspired to write legacy letters before now, consider your experience of the pandemic to be your entrée into this important work. Decades and generations from now, your experiences and values will resonate in a personal, meaningful, and perhaps useful way because you took the time to write and share.

I remember when the idea of a health crisis first became newsworthy. I recollect watching the national news as the deadly virus traveled around the world, moving closer to the United States, and I clearly recall when it was formally declared "a pandemic". The range of precautions suggested to the public were daunting and their efficacy uncertain. It seemed like a long time before there was a vaccine and the isolation and waiting were difficult for most of us and impossible for others. There ensued raging political and scientific debates. It was scary. It was complicated. It changed our lives in many ways. Reflecting on all of this has value and is worthy of content in our legacy letters.

Yes, there are "things," heirlooms I plan to leave each of our grandkids, but, in my heart, the three albums of legacy letters will be the most important. Duplicating one set of letters three times and placing them in each book has become the most significant "leaving" of all!

By sharing our stories, values and experiences, the next generations are able to learn about what our life was like (good and bad) in a very personal way, giving them detailed insight. We may choose to share about topics they never thought about or knew were important to us and would be to them. Our letters may lead them to new areas of interest, experience or study, inspiring them to learn something or pursue something they had never before considered. Ultimately, our stories are the only way we can form deeper connections as humans. Our legacy letters enable our heirs to truly understand us at a deeper level, which is an authentic, personal, and lasting gift.

Foreward

By Daniel Taylor

Author of *Creating a Spiritual Legacy: How to Share Your Stories, Values, and Wisdom*

Human beings are story-formed and story-telling creatures. Our brain is wired to look for a plot in the huge streams of data that enter it every moment. It makes stories from those streams because they are necessary both for survival and for flourishing. The most significant information, and the curated and applied information we call wisdom, is passed from person to person and from generation to generation through stories. Rachael Freed understands this profoundly and practically. She is a master teacher and facilitates us to utilize the art of turning our personal experiences into stories that benefit both ourselves and others.

The personal and collective experience that is the focus of this book is the Covid era--one that literally changed our collective lives (ending many), and she emphasizes, is still with us. It is with us literally in that mutations of the virus continue to sicken us, but perhaps even more importantly because the psychological and spiritual effects of the experience are carried in us and need to be explored and expressed—in stories–both to heal us and to protect us from similar dangers in the future.

Rachael Freed believes that secrets can be harmful. By keeping secrets about painful events from ourselves and others, we miss the healing and growth that is possible when such events are shared and worked out in collaboration with others–one other or a community of others.

One thing too many people kept secret during Covid–and to this day–is grief. Millions around the world died. Almost everyone knew of someone who died during the height of the pandemic. Of course, grief was acknowledged and sometimes expressed, but too often it was not, and is not. The single best way to grieve is to reflect on and tell the stories that convey our experience.

Freed advocates a specific form of storytelling that grows out of the Jewish tradition–the ethical will–that she calls legacy letters. Essentially, these are letters to people you care about that tell stories of significant life events, reflect on those stories in search of insight and wisdom, and offer that wisdom and the simple fact of valuing the recipient as a blessing. Legacy letters are a particular storytelling vehicle that blesses both the writer and the receiver.

The book is filled with examples from people of every age, relating their experience during the Covid era. These stories (in prose and poetry) explore a range of Covid experiences and reactions, from debilitating fear to dealing with intense grief at the loss of loved ones, to responding to isolation, to expressions of determination to be strong, to experiencing new creativity, to finding a growing determination to be of service to others. And there are responses that include gratitude for things that happened during this time as well.

Life and Loss: Legacy Writing in the Age of Covid–19 offers lessons from history that compare the Covid era with other pandemics and times of staggering loss: the Spanish Flu, the polio and AIDS crises, and the Holocaust. Freed finds parallels among them all, including undealt–with grief, silence, secret keeping, denial, and bureaucratic failure. We need to learn from these–including from Covid–to do better to save lives in the future. One important way to do so is to reflect on and tell our stories.

Fortunately, Rachael Freed doesn't just tell you to and give you her own and others' examples. She shows you how to do it yourself, step-by-step. The book concludes with practical exercises, prompts and guidelines for writing a legacy letter. She emphasizes the importance of this very human endeavor, describing the benefits derived from telling our stories, grieving, and building resilience.

So, get started! Someone you love needs your stories, and so do you

"God created humans because God loves stories."

– Elie Wiesel

Introduction: Breaking the Silence

We are all shaped by what we don't consciously know. As you read my story, consider your own family's secrets—and how they may have affected you.

My mother's older sister, Lillian, died at age 15 from the Spanish flu during the 1918 pandemic. I can only imagine the trauma this brought to my mother's family: three older siblings, her parents, and my mother, who was just three years old—too young to understand death or grief, but certainly not too young to feel its silent impact. As the baby of the family, she would have sensed the joy disappear from the household, absorbed the solemn mood, and experienced the shift, without knowing why.

Years later, I learned that after Lillian's death, my grandmother Minnie spent her days sitting on a bench at Lillian's grave. Her grief must have rippled through the family. I know it shaped her eldest daughter, Reva, who quit school after sixth grade to care for her younger siblings, including my mother and uncle.

What struck me most is that neither Lillian nor the pandemic was ever mentioned in family stories, not once. A catastrophe that claimed 675,000 lives in the U.S. alone, and it was as if it had never happened. As if Lillian had never existed.

A century later, I ask: how did that traumatic silence affect my mother, my aunts and uncles...and my generation? Could my grandmother's depression have contributed to my mother's depression? To my sister's? Both died prematurely. Could that unspoken grief still echo in us, the second generation?

I understand that in my grandmother's superstitious world, speaking of death was taboo. But avoiding it came at a cost, unprocessed trauma that I believe affected our family's mental health for decades.

We know little about how people truly suffered in the Spanish flu pandemic. No oral histories. No letters. No preserved grief. No lessons passed down. And when COVID-19 arrived in 2020, we were unprepared...not just logistically, but emotionally and spiritually.

In her 1992 book, *A Chorus of Stones,* Susan Griffin writes about the destructive power of secrecy and the healing power of truth:

> "I am beginning to believe that we know everything, that all history, including the history of each family, is part of us, such that when we hear any secret revealed, a secret about a grandfather, or an uncle, or a secret about the battle of Dresden* in 1945, our lives are made suddenly clearer to us, as the unnatural heaviness of unspoken truth is dispersed."

*I'd never heard of Dresden until I read Kurt Vonnegut's "novel" *Slaughterhouse* Five fifty-five years after the war. It is only one of the secrets omitted from our history books that make our country look like innocent heroes of WWII.

Echoes of hidden events, like the ripple effect of a stone on water, reverberate through generations whether we acknowledge them or not. Griffin argues, "It is our duty as humans to acknowledge these hurts, using this knowledge to create a better future."

Her words helped me understand the damage caused by my family's silence after Lillian's death. No one was invited to share their fears or grief. And that silence… passed down… became part of me too!

Why am I writing this book?

I didn't know it then, but I was on the edge of a life transition when the 21st century arrived. Since 1995, I'd been exploring a tradition known as the ethical will: ancient letters written by Jewish men to bless their sons, pass down values to the next generation, and share personal wishes about their dying and death.

In the summer of 1999, at a retreat, I had an experience that changed everything. In a seminar about ethical wills, I heard a voice. I'd never heard "a voice" before that moment, and it would be 24 years until I heard the voice again . . . a voice that guided and chided me. The voice, soft but sure, clear, gentle, feminine. She said just eight words that changed the direction and purpose of my life: "Turn this into a healing tool for women."

Startled, I raised my hand and shared what I'd heard. The rabbi–teacher pointed his finger at me and said, "Do it! It's an important niche."

And I did! I left my career as a psychotherapist and began modernizing and feminizing the ethical will: making it more accessible, current and relevant, especially for women.

Because the ethical will (a will of values) was neither a well-known term nor an approachable one, I changed its name to "legacy letters". I made many adaptations, but I always honored the three ancient principles: passing values forward, blessing the letter's recipients, and expressing final wishes.

For the next 25 years I taught, facilitated workshops and wrote books about legacy writing. Facilitating women to discover and share their voices in writing became my purpose.

Eventually, I began winding down, preparing for retirement. I trained facilitators to carry the work forward, declined more speaking invitations, and made peace with stepping back.

But then… COVID-19 happened.

Three years into the pandemic . . . while recovering from the virus myself I heard the voice again, the same voice I'd greeted once before, 24 years earlier. This time she said, "You're not done yet." My response was, "Oh s***!" watching my retirement plans evaporate before my eyes. I should have known that "humans plan and God laughs".

The voice calmly continued . . . "You still have one more book to write: a book inviting people to process and preserve their experiences of the COVID-19 era through legacy writing.

She was right! So here I am and I'm glad you're here too.

This Book Is For You!

This book is an invitation for you, people of all ages and genders, to break your silence. To explore, express, and reflect on your pandemic experience: your loneliness, loss, grief, resilience, growth, and transformation.

We'll examine not just what happened, but how it felt. How we changed. What we learned. And how we might carry these learnings forward: for our own healing, and for the generations to come.

The lines below the reflections, poems and legacy letters are for your use. Jot your responses, memories, and ideas beneath the contributors' offerings so you won't forget them.

Here's what to expect:

- **Chapter 1** looks at the early days of the pandemic and includes the importance of community, and legacy reflections written during that time.

- **Chapter 2** explores how we coped with change, including isolation, loneliness and forgetting.

- **Chapter 3** focuses on grief and death, highlighting the groundbreaking work of Susan Griffin about secrets, and Pauline Boss' illumination of ambiguous loss.

- **Chapter 4** deepens the dimensions of grief, the growth of resilience.

– **Chapter 5** introduces the unexpected gifts of the pandemic.

- **Appendix I** provides historical context, pandemics past and present. We are not alone!

- **Appendix II** presents the history of the Legacy Letter (Ethical Will) from biblical times.

- **Appendix III** offers a legacy writing exercise: looking at how you coped.

- **Appendix IV** shares practical tips and tools for Legacy Letter Writing.

- **Appendix V** a repeat from chapter 1: a template of the four basic elements of a Legacy Letter.

- **Appendix VI** gives last minute suggestions as you begin your First Covid Legacy Letter.

- **Appendix G** is a curated reading list for those interested in pandemic fiction.

This book is about memory, meaning, and the legacy of lived experience: what we remember, what we need to remember, and what we must pass on.

Our perceptions of the world changed daily during the pandemic and many people came to realize that we can create a new reality and gratitude for life. Once expressed, we can convey our learnings to future generations, so they will not be as unprepared and naïve as we've been when the next pandemic raises its deadly head.

This book is a legacy for you. Writing is a healing tool. It can unlock your grief, build resilience, reawaken creativity, and open your heart again.

"Perhaps what is wanted in our own dark, anti-truth times ...
is a literature of personal history and reflection:
direct, authentic, scrupulous about fact."
– Sigrid Nunez, author of *The Vulnerables*

You and I are blessed by the writings in this book: reflections, stories, letters, and poems, by diverse people who have shared their work to enrich our understanding and appreciation of the range of pandemic experiences. Along the way, you'll hear from contributors, writing from across the U.S., Canada, and Mexico.

We begin with three poems that mark the opening of this pandemic era in human history. The first by Rutha Rosen is a short and powerful example of the fears we faced followed by Sarah Bourns Crosby's challenges and exposures, and Kitty O'Meara's hope and hints of healing.

Together, they set the tone for what's to come.

COVID- Three Days In

By Rutha Rosen

"An elderly woman

struggles to pack her vegetables

into a canvas tote

I hear her cry out for assistance

but I am frozen

as if the very thought

of turning to help

had transformed me

into a pillar of salt."

We've All Been Exposed

by Sarah Bourne Crosby

https://sarahbournscrosby.com

"We've all been exposed.
Not necessarily to the virus
(though maybe...who knows).

We've all been exposed BY the virus.
Corona is exposing us.
Exposing our weak sides.
Exposing our dark sides.

Exposing what normally lays far beneath the surface of our souls,
hidden by the invisible masks we wear.
Now exposed by the paper masks we can't hide far enough behind.

Corona is exposing our addiction to comfort.
Our obsession with control.
Our compulsion to hoard.
Our protection of self.

Corona is peeling back our layers.
Tearing down our walls.
Revealing our illusions.
Leveling our best-laid plans.

Corona is exposing the gods we worship:
Our health
Our hurry
Our sense of security

Our favorite lies
Our secret lusts
Our misplaced trust.

Corona is calling everything into question:
What is the church without a building?
What is my worth without an income?
How do we plan without certainty?
How do we love despite risk?
Corona is exposing me.
My mindless numbing
My endless scrolling
My careless words
My fragile nerves.

We've all been exposed.

Our junk laid bare.
Our fears made known.

The band-aid torn.

The masquerade done.

So, What now? What's left?

Clean hands

Clear eyes

Tender hearts."

Following Crosby's inquiry of our souls, we turn to a poem that evokes hope. "In the Time of Pandemic" by Kitty O'Meara became an early touchstone for many… a vision of stillness, healing, and possibility.

O'Meara later published a picture book of the same title (Tra Pu blishing, 2020), presenting her message to children aged 4-8.

In the Time of Pandemic

Kitty O'Meara

"And the people stayed home.

And read books, and listened, and rested, and exercised, and made art, and played games, and learned new ways of being and were still.

And listened more deeply. Some meditated, some prayed, some danced. Some met their shadows. And the people began to think differently.

And the people healed.

And, in the absence of people living in ignorant, dangerous, mindless, and heartless ways, the earth began to heal.

And when the danger passed, and the people joined together again, they grieved their losses, and made new choices, and dreamed new images, and created new ways to live and heal the earth fully, as they had been healed."

Stories and stones have a deeper impact on people than instructions, I began with a personal story about my Aunt Lillian in the introduction and I begin with another here to engage your heart and inspire your own histories, grief and learning, during our most recent pandemic.

Chapter 1: Let's Begin at the Beginning

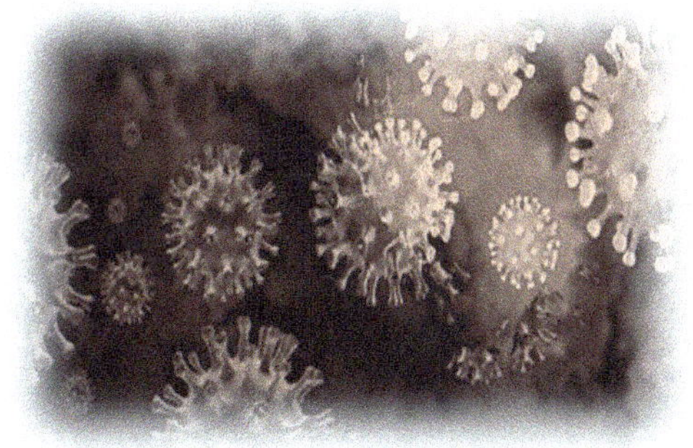

"Tell me and I forget.

Teach me and I remember.

Involve me and I learn."

– Benjamin Franklin

Reflections from 2020

My experience of the early days of the pandemic began two months before our country was officially shut down in mid-March of 2020. I spent those months in Jaffa, Israel, where I lived in a beautiful old guest house appropriately named the "Secret Garden". The garden and guest house were separated from the street by a high wall...privacy common in the Middle East.

> "My time there was, I thought then, the beginning of my life as a retiree. Having worked from the age of twelve, I was finding it a difficult transition. I had no schedule and could make of my days whatever I chose. But what and how to choose?
>
> "Each morning, I shopped around the corner at an Arab family's tiny shop that sold what was considered the best hummus in Israel. Buying it and their freshly baked pita that I added to my juicy oranges and vegetables at home, I prepared a leisurely breakfast. I wish you could have smelled the garlic and tasted the pita, still warm from the oven; it makes my mouth water as I write about it today.
>
> "Outside in the secret garden, I ate in the dappled sunlight, reading every morning from a 2007 book, *City of Oranges: An Intimate History of Arabs and Jews in Jaffa*, by Adam LeBora.
>
> "Every other morning, I snapped a photo of a white orchid growing on the terrace as together we were nourished by the Mediterranean sun and breeze.

"We grew together, the orchid from tiny bulb to full flower, and me in gratitude for everything: from the delicious fresh food, the serenity and unfamiliar quiet of little traffic noise beyond the walls, to the dappled morning sun, clean air and gentle breeze, the birds' songs, and the peace of the dew nurturing the emerging garden.

"An extrovert all my life, I was beginning to learn about flowering in quiet, in contemplation, in appreciation: in not frantically "doing" all the time.

"When my magical months were over, I flew home, from Tel Aviv to Minneapolis, changing planes in Toronto the evening of March 14, 2020. The Toronto International airport, usually bustling with duty-free shoppers, was eerily quiet at 8:30 PM.

"When my connecting plane landed safely in Minneapolis, I discovered that not only was I beginning a 14-day quarantine (as a result of flying internationally), but that my flight from Tel Aviv was the last one out of Israel, and my Toronto flight was the last one permitted into the US. No wonder the Toronto airport was so quiet!

"The worldwide pandemic COVID-19 had officially begun!

"I sensed sliding doors slamming shut, as I slipped from one world into another, from carefree freedom to a lengthy lockdown.

"That spring and summer I spent learning new skills to keep myself safe. Most days I spent at home, going out only rarely, socially distancing when I did, and always masked. I kept busy washing, washing, washing: my hands, my door handles, my groceries, my dishes, my countertops, my bedding, my bathroom, my clothes. I worried about the safety of my family, others I knew and myself. My pre-Jaffa routine didn't work nor did my newly discovered Jaffa habits. I had to construct a new daily plan, but I continued to contemplate retirement.

"Privileged to own a computer, a smart phone, a TV and to know how to use Zoom, I could communicate with others all over the world although I lived alone in my apartment.

"I heard about health workers called to work double shifts because there weren't enough staff to cover the growing number of patients, getting sick themselves because their protective clothing was insufficient (and looked as if it'd been 'borrowed' from outer space). I heard about medication and medical equipment shortages, patients housed in hospital hallways because rooms had overflowed, emergency tent hospitals being built, stadiums and event spaces being converted into hospitals, and rows of refrigerated trucks holding and hiding the dead until they could be identified and buried.

"It was sad, terrifying, horrifying, and confusing. I'd never seen death so vast and widespread, affecting the whole planet. I was confused to hear President Trump say, "It's going to disappear. one day—it's like a miracle—it will disappear," while I simultaneously watched news reporting that pandemic numbers were escalating. By mid-October 220,000 Americans had died from COVID-19 and by October 31, 2020, there was an average of 81,737 new cases daily in the United States.

"The confusion led me to consider that one explanation for the global political movement to the right, to dictators who claimed to be able to magically solve all our problems, "just give me the power", was a result of individual vulnerability and personal powerlessness as we were exposed to the chaos and mass death reported by the media daily. I extrapolated from this idea that often young people who have no power or control over parental or sexual abuse tend to be attracted to cults or religious orthodoxy. There they are promised security and protection if the rules are 'religiously' performed.

"At 82, I began to think seriously about what I would want if I were dying of COVID-19. This led me to rewrite a portion of my living will. After I consulted with my physician (via Zoon), I wrote to my children and felt relieved and more secure."

A Brief Addendum to my Health Care Directive

"To my beloved children, Sid (Shlomi) and Debbie:

If I contract COVID-19 as part of the worldwide pandemic and need to be hospitalized, and subsequently need assistance to breathe, I want the following:

First, I want respiratory assistance (oxygen from a nasal cannula, e.g. a flexible tube inserted into the nostrils).

Second, I do NOT want mechanical respiration if my brain can no longer sustain my own breathing.

If my body is not recovering with the assistance of oxygen with the nasal cannula, please follow my wishes (no respirator) and allow me to die peacefully, keeping me as comfortable as possible with medication.

My decision was made after consultation with my physician (on 4-28-2020 via Zoom). We discussed my good physical, emotional, and mental health as well as my age and spiritual values, my attitudes and choices about extending life, palliative care, as well as the unknown short-and-long-term effects of mechanical respiration.

I know having to accede to my wishes will be difficult, and I hope you won't have to, and I'm truly sorry if you do. Please know that I love you more than I ever will be able to express and have so much gratitude for the care and love you have given me over the years and to this day.

Please consider this addendum as part of my signed directive, written and signed while I remain healthy and free of COVID-19.

Rachael Freed April 28, 2020"

____

____

____

____

____

Here is a quite different response from an elder, a poignant meditation from spring 2020 from the author of *Twilight Time: Aging in Amazement*, Susie Kaufman. This word picture, titled "Take Heart" thoughtful, witty, and deeply observant, is of experiencing COVID-19 with her sister who suffers undiagnosed dementia.

> "Some of us see a dark future or no future, a lunar wasteland replacing the paradise we have only recently come to notice. Some of us see a renaissance, a flowering of art and justice replicating itself in all directions and dimensions like a hall of mirrors. And some of us can't make up our minds.
>
> "My sister sat in her recliner and took it all in..... We fortified ourselves with cashews. We did our trademark imaginary tour of upper Broadway, seeing if we could remember all the stores and all the shopkeepers from the fifties. Every morning, my sister read the dire headlines in the *Chronicle*.
>
> "I explained that there was a virus like a wildfire in the Sierras spreading out of control all over the world and she nodded. I

couldn't tell if it registered, if it meant anything. But then again what did it mean to us? No more Thai food? No more browsing and people-watching at the bookstore? It's not like a terrorist attack. It dawns on you slowly, each new day.

"At first, I kissed her forehead each time I entered her room and each time I left, marking the coming and going as if my sister were a mezuzah holding a sacred text. And maybe she is and maybe I am and maybe you are. But in the last days of the trip, I no longer kissed my people. We communicated our love for one another virtually, sometimes in words, but more often in chaste adoring glances like shy Victorians. I put my hand to my heart and she put her hand to her heart.

"When I sat opposite her on the final day before heading to the airport with my N95 mask and my supply of blue plastic gloves, she was leaning back in her chair under a wool blanket. She reached out from under the weight of it and grabbed my pinky finger with her pinky finger. We made a pinky promise, the way schoolgirls do, and despite the potential contagion of her skin touching my skin, we promised to love one another no matter the wreckage of this broken world."

____

____

____

____

____

As author Susie Kaufman reflected about the earliest days of the pandemic with her sister in spring 2020, Susanna Schuerman, a senior legacy writing facilitator from Iowa, wrote a spiritual reflection in autumn, 2020. She titled it:

"What is it the season for?"

By *Susanna Schuerman*

"Iowa is richly blessed with the fragrances, sights and sounds of each turning season. Autumn is especially conducive to contemplative walks in the woods. A canopy of colors showers me with crimson, amber and burnt orange as leaves fall into a new becoming.

"Maples and oaks surrender their hold allowing leaves to flutter into compost. Autumn is a time of letting go of what no longer serves us. Attuning to the rhythms of the seasons can be a wisdom guide to teach us about life's rise and fall—like the ebb and flow of the tides and the waxing and waning of the moon.

"What is it the season for? The rise of the pandemic has triggered a season of social unrest, a season of confronting our fears, a season of rethinking our values, a season of listening to our inner voices. This season is ripe for transformation. It's time to reap the harvest of summer's growth. What have I learned and how will it carry me into the quietude of winter and the greening of spring? As I continue my prayerful walk, I cast my eyes to the ground focusing on the rocky path I follow. It would be too easy to fall into despair, but just when it seems like everything is falling apart, that is precisely when I feel closest to the Divine. My hope and prayer are that without speaking a word, the light within me will urge me to bestow blessings on those who pass by, both human and non-human.

"As I reach the top of the hill, my eyes are drawn upward to the vastness of the blue sky, to the treetops and then to the river that flows below. I feel less isolated with this wider view. I breathe deeply the crisp, cool air. I feel connected to all of life through breath, through air that envelops the entire Earth. I listen to this invisible element that invites me to release control of my narrow views—to listen with my whole body. What are the black bodies, the brown bodies, the white bodies, all bodies, trying to say during these turbulent times? A wise sage once said that to listen is to risk being changed forever.

"Is it possible for me to me to put down my books, stop reading about love and kindness, and instead, open to the spirit within and listen—really listen to the stories of others.

"What is it the season for? When I, when we, as a nation, stop trying to shape all of humanity into our own image, to see past the divisions we create, open our eyes to the panoramic view and become still enough to listen…we will join as eager and willing participants in this new becoming.

"*(Becoming – when a leaf releases its hold from a branch and flutters to the ground, it will eventually become compost. It has a new purpose. So, when we release what no longer works for us, we can become something new, find a new purpose.)"

____

____

____

____

____

Susanna's reflection focused on nature helps us shift our attention from the individual to a larger focus, to community, to humanity, our next pandemic consideration.

Abigail Pogrebin, co-author of *It Takes Two to Torah,* wrote of her community concern in 2024 as Covid made it clear that although the pandemic affected everyone, suffering was greater in certain segments of our society:

> "People in poor communities without access to healthcare are unable to have COVID tests, people who don't have paid sick leave have to work to put food on the table and are the most endangered in the current reality; some kids go without lunch because they're not going to school; some people don't have access to the internet. A lot of the inequities and hardships of society come to the fore."

____

____

____

____

____

Building Community during the Pandemic

Beyond my own family, what do I know about us as Americans that hinders us from building and relying on community as a way of dealing with a pandemic?

One thing I know is that as a people we are independent often to the detriment of others. We don't want to be told what to do! We respect above almost anything, those who are materially successful on their own, "who pull themselves up by their own bootstraps," though I believe this is an American myth!

Another thing I know is that we were not educated about the history of pandemicsw so we were totally unprepared for COVID.

And still another thing I've observed is that, generally speaking, we repress or push away our fear of death. We are rarely willing to talk about it, or to permit expression of our feelings, our grief, which would allow us to build resilience and perhaps even heal.

In 2011 Anne K. Gross, PhD. wrote *The Polio Journals: Lessons from My Mother,* airing the 70-year-old secrets and silence kept by her family, that had restricted Anne and her daughters from grieving and healing:

> "My willingness to believe that my mother's paralysis was insignificant was a means of protecting myself from my own childhood scars brought on by growing up in a family bound by secrets, forbidden to express pain..... I realized too that the generational impact of polio did not stop with me, that the secrets surrounding my mother's disability affected my two daughters a s well. It was time to uncover the truth

about my mother's life.... my attempt to make sense of the legacy of my mother's illness and the price all of us paid for not speaking the truth."

____

____

____

____

____

Yet another thing I know about us (and maybe it's just me that I'm talking about): is that we enjoy our privilege, are self-centered and don't want to be inconvenienced by others. When the country shut down in March 2020 and we were told to stay in our houses away from others, not to go into crowds of people, to remember to wear a mask if we did go out, we felt beleaguered rather than protected.

Another thing I know, and this is undoubtedly psychologically true about all people, is that we want to forget the painful things in our lives. We wanted Covid to be over and we wanted not to have to think about it again, not to think about what we lost, not to think about what we learned, rather to pretend that it never happened.

As I write this in autumn of 2025, we still find variants of COVID-19 occurring, and in fact rising. New vaccines to handle the virus' variants continue to be developed and it's being advised that we again wear masks in public. This advice in 2025 comes after we were told by the CDC that the pandemic was over more than two years ago.

In his Substack column, *Ground Truths,* on August 23, 2023, Eric Topol, MD, cardiologist and professor of molecular medicine at Scripps Research, wrote:

> "Facing the fact that this virus, in one version or another,
> will be with us for many years to come, rather than
> denialism and complacency, is critical."

And in 2024 in the Los Angeles Times Dr. Topol was quoted, saying:

> "Now in its fifth year,
> SARS-CoV-2 has once again proved to be highly resilient,
> capable of reinventing itself to infect us.
> Yet we continue to make-believe that the pandemic is over,
> that infections have been transformed to common cold status
> by prior exposure(s), and that life has returned to normal.
> Sadly, none of this is true."

So, I know that we–as a nation–are eager to put COVID-19 behind us, out of our minds and hearts.

Yet I also know that most of us care for and love our children, and we want what's best for them. By sharing with them what we experienced throughout COVID-19, we may help them to deal better with whatever pandemic comes their way long after we are gone.

Supreme Court Justice, Ketanji Brown Jackson, wrote profoundly about the dangers of forgetting and failing to seek and disseminate knowledge to the next generations:

> "Knowledge emboldens people, and it frees them. The work of our time is maintaining that hard-won freedom. And to do that. . .we must teach it to our children and preserve it for theirs.... we can only know where we are, and where we're going, if we realize where we've been.
>
> "Knowledge of the past is what enables us to mark our forward progress. If we are going to continue to move forward as a nation, we cannot allow concerns about discomfort to displace knowledge, truth, or history.... the uncomfortable lessons are often the ones that teach us the most about ourselves...."

____

____

____

____

____

Learning from Journal Writing

Here are some of my journal entries begun in 2020 focused on nature as others have written, with gratitude, realizing that climate change could take nature's gifts from us, and my realization about how grateful I am for the simplest things in my life.

> "This spring perhaps more than any other, I've loved strolling in the park behind my home, watching newborn goslings swimming behind their mothers, delighting in the perennials pushing through the earth exposing their vibrant colors, surveying the grass greening, and being among the trees granting shade and serenity as they fill out and once again become home to the red-winged blackbirds and tiny brown wrens. I experience gratitude for my life most keenly when I'm outdoors."

However, a series of journal entries surprised me, showing how important community is to me, how much I am nourished by it, how it contributes to my need for belonging, and how much effort and time I've used to both create and participate in communities.

> "Since I self-quarantined after flying from Tel Aviv to Toronto amidst 359 other coughing passengers and on to Minneapolis I've been sequestered at home.
>
> "Living alone as I have for the past 30 years takes on new meaning as the days and weeks of "sheltering-in-place" crawl on.

"I am a natural extrovert and over my lifetime have sought 'family' and 'communities' to nourish them and support my soul too. Now I observe that my hunger and yearning for community grows bigger all the time. Could I be depressed? Why do I like sleeping so much and for so long?

"It didn't take much time for my family and communities to become adept (all ages) at using technology to gather. My Al-Anon group meets weekly on Zoom, as does my 'Wisdom Circle'. Our extended family and friends gather on Zoom to celebrate Passover. My synagogue provides services and classes on Zoom with the rabbis leading from their homes. (I wish I'd had the foresight to buy Zoom stock in March 2020!)"

Here I interrupt my journal to share a delightful poem by Laura Hammond that describes with humor how inept we all were about using Zoom at the beginning of the pandemic:

"Church ZOOM"

by Laura Hammond

"In the beginning you are fixated on your hair

wondering if your eyes always looked crossed

focusing on other people's ZOOM appropriate

business casual lounge wear.

Microphones pick up each

rustling paper or turning page

another sip of coffee or a cough

rendering the Pastor temporarily speechless.

Their phones ring.

They explain in several iterations

They are at church.

Couples turn their faces away from the camera

to have a whispering skirmish

what their lives must sound like every day.

We sing as a glorious chorus of one at a time

hoping it is someone who can hold a tune

or knows the hymn.

In the end we spend as much time saying goodbye

as we spent in the service

because no one knows how to turn it off."

And now back to my journal, to the entries that unearthed an important learning about myself: my need for community.

> "Unaware of my personal need, I initiated four small communities in 2020. My teen grandkids were "going to school" on Zoom. They awakened each morning, checked in with their teachers, did brief assignments, and had nothing to do for the rest of the day. So, I organized a 'book club' for them and me.
>
> "The second community began as I was organizing pictures one afternoon. I discovered a century old photo of my maternal grandparents and their first three children. Deciding to share it with my remaining six cousins (ages 60 to 92 living all over the country), I emailed it to them with an invitation to start a Zoom community to share how each of us is dealing with the pandemic. Enthusiastically received, we have now included our interested children, making the community intergenerational, and have planned a Zoom get together every six weeks (Some of us had not seen the others since we were children!)
>
> "The third community is still in progress. I emailed all the certified legacy facilitators whom I'd trained to come together on Zoom to share our selves and our work in legacy writing. (See their reflections about COVID-19 in the next chapter.) I hoped that this small professional community would be enriched beyond the personal writing

we'd share. That some of them would declare interest in taking over the facilitator training, so I could retire from that aspect of my work, relieved to know that legacy writing would continue to grow and spread.

"I realized the communities I'd created early in the pandemic were not only useful and supportive for others, young and old, but that it is part of my nature to build communities and to accept that communities fill my need to belong and feed my soul too."

"The earliest and most basic definition of community—of tribe—
would be the group of people that you would both
help feed and help defend.
A society that doesn't offer its members
the chance to act selflessly in these ways
isn't a society
in any tribal sense of the word...."

– Sebastian Junger, author of *Tribe*

"I'd been reading David Plouff's pre-pandemic book about how to participate in the 2022 election. He'd written that if everyone could get five people to register, we would have done our part. I recognized that I might be able to make registration simple for the residents in my condo building by providing them with voter registration forms and mail-in ballots.

"There'd been substantial turnover in recent years, and the population in the 131 units had become significantly younger. I emailed my building manager for p ermission; he though t it was 'a great idea' and I called the city. They sent over sets of reg istration and mail-in vot ing forms for the July 2022 primary.

"Here was my simple plan: I'd deliver the forms to everyone's door with a cover sheet that said, 'Delivered to you by a masked and gloved fellow resident.' That seemed safe for them and me and doubled as my exercise on days when rain kept me from the park.

"In May 2024, again on my dining room table, were a pile of voter registration forms and mail-in primary ballots. I waited for a rainy day to make the sun shine again to do my part for the community."

Simplifying Writing a Legacy Letter

Some years ago, I developed a template to guide beginning legacy letter writers. The letter focuses on just four elements: The opening paragraph sets the *context* of the letter; the second tells a *story*, a reflection, or a meaningful experience; the third extracts the lesson, *learning or values* from the story…your wisdom; and the fourth paragraph is a *blessing* for the recipient(s) of the letter, (key content from the original ethical will).

Following the template I'll share one legacy letter I wrote, using reflections from my journal, and organizing my message using the template. First, here is the template with explanation.

A Template for Writing a Legacy Letter

1. *A context-setting paragraph*
2. *A story or reflection*
3. *A lesson, value or insight–your wisdom*
4. *A closing blessing*

This simple yet profound structure helps guide your writing and brings coherence, order and meaning to your letter. No matter the content a template provides a structure, making writing legacy letters simpler and less daunting. A legacy letter using this framework can often be completed in four paragraphs in about 30 minutes. Feel free to use this as a guide and adapt it to your own voice and purpose:

Paragraph 1: Context

A wise mentor once told me, "All texts have a context." We are often unaware of the broader influences shaping our lives. Offering a framework for what follows gives your readers a snippet of family history, a snapshot of significant present and historical times, a meaningful frame for what follows, and provides depth to your personal reflection.

Paragraph 2: Story

All of us have unique stories, deeply personal and shaped by our time. Sharing them helps us feel seen and known, creates belonging, connects us to past and future generations, and allows us to pass forward the insights and wisdom we've acquired. The story may recount a personal experience, an ancestral memory, a cherished tradition or ritual, an apology, appreciation, or a major event like the COVID-19 pandemic. Use vivid details to make your story come alive. Your letter need not contain every story, just one that matters right now.

Paragraph 3: Learning

This is where wisdom emerges. Reflect on the insight, value, or learning gained from your story. What personal truth will you pass forward? This is often the most meaningful part of the legacy letter, where your experience is transformed into a legacy, a lasting gift for those who come after you.

Paragraph 4: Blessing

Offer a heartfelt blessing. This closing paragraph flows naturally from your story and reflection. It may include words of encouragement, protection, hope, or affirmation. As we bless others, we often find ourselves blessed as well.

The ancient ethical will (from which contemporary legacy letters are derived) originated from the biblical story of Jacob, who, before his death, blessed his twelve sons (Genesis 49). This is the same Jacob who once stole his father Isaac's blessing from his older brother, Esau. One of the most poignant moments in Genesis (27:38) is Esau's cry to his father:

"Have you but one blessing, my father? Bless me, even me also…
And Esau lifted up his voice and wept."

We never outgrow our need for blessing.

 Adapted from *Your Legacy Matters*

My COVID Letter to the Future

Here is one of my legacy letters about COVID-19 and me written when I was 84. It's addressed to future generations whom I may never meet. Using reflections from my 2020 journal, I shaped it with the four-paragraph template.

"Dear future family,

(Context)

I'm writing to you about 2020 when the COVID-19 pandemic began to change our world. I think it's important to know about pandemics, even though our family survived.

My Aunt Lillian, my mother's 15-year-old sister, died of the Spanish Flu in 1918. More people died in that Pandemic than died in WWI and WWII combined. Archived records indicate 500 million people were infected worldwide, and one third of the world's population, 50 million, died from the Spanish flu. It was taboo to speak of death in that time (and somewhat true today). I have no records or stories about my Aunt Lillian, nor how my mother's life and the life of her family were affected.

In America in 2020 alone, 365,000 died from COVID-19, and over one million died in the first four years. Beyond each death, there is a story of a life, and of a grieving family. It is important to hear, remember and learn from these stories, and that's why I'm writing you today. Of course, I can only tell you my own stories.

I began sheltering-at-home on March 14, 2020, when I returned by plane from Israel. The pandemic arrived in the US a few days later in all its deadly strength. The country (and the larger world) shut down, and we began "sheltering-in-place".

(Story/Experience)

Recently during Covid, I noticed that when I have something purposeful to accomplish, I feel fine. An example is that for over twenty years I had dedicated an afternoon every week to read books for Minnesota Radio Talking Book for the blind. I love reading aloud and was glad to be able to share books with those who could not read. That halted abruptly as everyone stayed at home. Days when I have nothing on my calendar, it's harder to function, even to get out of bed, easier to numb myself with tv, junk food, and naps. It's more difficult to focus on reading, even fiction.

I'd always read to my seven grandkids and now as they were starting various years of high school, their classes were online because of the pandemic. They got up in the morning: checked in with their teachers and sometimes were given short assignments: their education was brief and inadequate. They had nothing to do for the rest of the day and no social contacts. I was appalled!

So, I organized a "book club" for them; I read to them as I had when they were young non-readers. We met twice a week for 45 minutes (the only regular structure they had) on Zoom and after I read to them, discussion followed and then socializing among the cousins. We started with *The Fire Next Time* which seemed appropriate because George Floyd, an innocent black man, had been murdered by a police officer in May of 2020 in our very own city, Minneapolis, spawning national protests. After that we tackled a Holocaust novel, *The Book Thief.*

Then something magical happened. My granddaughter Lily, to whom I'd been reading for her whole life, suggested it was time to switch roles, that she wanted to read to me. (Amazing!) A few weeks later, her brother Harry told me he didn't want to "cut in on Lily's gig", but he'd like to read to me too. Then the biggest miracle of all: my 52-year-old son, called me saying he didn't want to interject himself into my relationship with his kids, but he'd like to read to me too!

What more could an 82-year-old mother/grandmother ask for? I now have three weekly appointments when each of them not only reads to me, but we discuss many things, and they tell me about their lives…all on Zoom, an early online miracle that's become widely available for people to communicate and see each other on screens all over the world.

(Learning/Values)

My reflection might make you think that COVID-19 wasn't a problem but death surrounded all of us. The park, housing life, and my Zoom connections fed my spirit, but it didn't really make my total life less lonely. Our world as we knew it was no more; everything had shut down: no restaurants open, no theater nor movies, no concerts, no baseball games, no meeting friends for coffee. I had to find support within myself–about which I knew little. because I was a natural extrovert. Habitually I'd relied on my social life and had focused outward throughout my life. But even that difficulty provided me with an opportunity: to discover my internal resilience, to grieve what was lost, to rebuild my life, relying more on my core strengths and what I could give to others. I realized the gifts of reading helped and that reading aloud to others–and being read to by my beloveds–nourished me and them as we shared Zoom contact.

Reading, that I've loved since elementary school, had a purpose beyond my own joy and learning: to help my grandkids in such a challenging time. Beyond the social and intellectual stimulation that reading provided them was stability, something to look forward to regularly and a sense that reading could enlarge their perspectives about the world beyond their shut–in spaces. That my grandkids and son are still reading to me is a splendid and unexpected gift of Covid.

(Blessing)

My dear great grandchildren,

Should you ever be in a similar situation (and I pray you won't), I hope that knowing how I lived in the first years of COVID-19 will open doors fitting your skills and interests to share with others. Allowing yourself to grieve, openly and fully, will open your hearts to the gifts of our world and be a legacy gift to your own children and grandchildren. Beyond the pandemic, I bless you, like your forebears, with the love of reading, and hope that books (in whatever form they present themselves in your generation) will enrich and expand your lives.

Blessings of love and resilience to each of you,

Your great grandmother– Rachael"

____

____

____

____

____

A senior legacy writing facilitator, Michael Ziomko, shared his powerful 2024 letter to his daughter Kara, expressing his hope for community as the lesson and blessing of COVID-19:

"My dear Kara,

Now that my covid is winding down I'm feeling stronger, but it's made me think about the pandemic and how lucky I am to be alive. It also brought back a particular memory from early in the pandemic, a story I want to tell you, because it reflects my concerns about our country and our ability going forward to make a good and accepting nation for all.

As I was retiring in the summer of 2020 and cleaning out my office, I spent about a week carrying trash to the dumpster in the alley, where several neighbors from next door gathered to smoke, given the no-smoking rules where they lived. There was one man who consistently complained about the rule requiring him to wear a mask when he was outside his room. Endlessly he would rant: "I have rights! You can't make me wear a mask!"

This was early in the pandemic – before we knew that over a million people would die and so many others suffer lifelong illness. But in his mind, all that was important was that 'he had rights'! It made me think about our country and its absolute embrace of the value of individualism. We're told: Go out and make something of yourself! Pick yourself up and do better! Pull yourself up by your own bootstraps! But what about making something together? What about looking out for one another? No, it's about 'me!' and 'me' alone. Let other people look out for themselves. It's not my fault if they can't make something of their lives!

I'm not thinking of this from a religious point of view, just a humanitarian one. I'm 75, and all I've ever heard is, 'Go out and make something of yourself!' It's never been about making community, looking out for and helping others and finding your own happiness within and as a part of the happiness of your community.

I think we can see that so clearly in the political drama that is unfolding. I understand that individualism is a key part of free enterprise, and free enterprise is a core value of this country. Freedom equals individualism in the American experience – and it seems clear to me that freedom and individualism cannot include community. To wear a mask early in the pandemic, and even now, means you're thinking of others; you don't want them to get Covid in case you have it as much as you don't want to get it from them if they have it.

Back to the man at the trash cannister: he has rights, and you can't tell him what to do. It doesn't seem to occur to him that what he does might hurt others, or even himself. It doesn't occur to him to think about others first. Not hurting others isn't a core value, nor is helping others and looking out for them a core value.

If the pandemic has taught us anything I hope it is this: that we live and thrive best when we do it together, with each other, leaning on and supporting each other. But my sadness is - and the lesson from the pandemic is - that I don't see how that value will ever be embraced. It's not that it doesn't happen in individual circumstances; it's just that it is not a community-wide value.

We must talk about this. We must act. Before it is too late.

I love you, Kara, and I know that in your own life the value of loving others, looking out for others, and doing for others is how you live. I give you all my blessings to support the enduring legacy of your life of love, caring, and beauty - despite all that surrounds us.

Your father, Michael"

I'm not sure where I found this poster, but it spoke to me of generosity, kindness and community.

I WEAR MY MASK IN PUBLIC FOR THREE REASONS:

1. HUMILITY: I don't know if I have COVID as it is clear that people can spread the disease before they have symptons.
2. KINDNESS: I don't know if the person I am near has a child battling cancer, or cares for their elderly mom. While I might be fine, they might not.
3. COMMUNITY: I want my community to thrive, businesses to stay open, employees to stay healthy. Keeping a lid on COVID helps us all!

This pandemic reflection by my dear friend, Martha Albrecht, an extraordinary community servant, speaks of her loss of community. She passed in January 2023.

> "In January 2020 I watched with pity as people in China were forced to wear masks. In late February realizing I'd soon be wearing one, I bought toilet paper, frozen fruits and vegetables and bags of coffee. Then, on March 11, my sister called to say her daughter, who works for the MN Dept. of Public Health, told her that she and her siblings (we were all high risk) needed to stay in place. Period.
>
> "It was cold in Minnesota so outdoor gatherings with masks and social distancing came later. My immediate tasks were to make sure my will and medical directive

were current. In the days that followed I cleaned drawers and closets so that my kids and sisters wouldn't think poorly of me. Then came the harder part … learning to live in the new reality.

"The greatest blessing was that COVID-19 arrived in a time of iPhones, computers, Zoom and FaceTime. I missed hugging my kids and grandkids, but I could still see them and talk with them virtually. I reconnected with friends by phone instead of talking over lunch. I even sent my grandkids silly old videos from my iPad.

"My lifeline to sanity now offers Zoom AA meetings that include people attending a meeting for the first time without the fear of 'walking into their first meeting' and the benefit of being 'totally anonymous'. That change was profound.

"I'd been bringing AA and Al-Anon Meetings to the Shakopee Women's Correctional Facility since 2000 and all contact came to a sudden halt. The absence of these women in my life left a hole in my heart.

"Then came May 26th when the George Floyd video was released and the police brutality and racism in Minnesota was exposed. There was something surreal about watching CNN and other media on the streets of our city as the "Black Lives Matter" peaceful protests began and then others turned the rights and nights into riots and looting and fires. I wept — for George Floyd, for our city, for our illusions.

"But I also prayed and hoped that this is not a moment in time, but rather a time of real movement and change. John Lewis passed the baton as he left us. Women and men of good faith have picked it up and are coming together to address and end systemic racism.

"There is much to be grateful for in this upside-down world.

"My dog Benji hangs on my every word; he's a constant source of joy and comfort. Sorting old photos and a lifetime of memories that go with them bring tears or smiles and both are welcome.

"I'm blessed with and grateful for family, for friends, and for being able to enjoy my own company. I even found a card explaining myself to me. It's framed on my desk. "I never realized how funny I was until I started talking to myself."

____

____

____

____

____

You likely noticed Martha's reference to George Floyd's murder on May 26, 2020. The surprise and shame we Minneapolitans experienced was palpable. We naïvely thought Minneapolis was different! Rev. Al Sharpton, who led Floyd's memorial service, suggested that we stand to experience how long nine plus minutes really is. It was almost unbearable to stand silent and still, for the amount of time that the officer's knee pressed on Floyd's neck and killed him. Although COVID was rampant, many hundreds of thousands of black, brown, and white people came together to march as one community throughout the world, reawakened to the prevalent and persistent racism in our country.

Bill Marsella, like Michael Ziomko, a senior legacy writing facilitator, wrote this legacy letter to his grandchildren in June 2020, titled The Fire Next Time. He, like so many others, felt the fire of righteous grief, and saw, even then, a flame of hope. The shameful act of George Floyd's murder awakened us yet again to America's systemic racism, a pandemic that complicated all our lives during the first summer of COVID-19.

> "My dear family,
>
> It is no accident that we experienced the murder of George Floyd at the hands of the police - and the protests and riots that ensued which literally burned parts of our beloved City of Minneapolis to the ground - while we are undergoing a world-wide pandemic. Moments in history like this 'leave a legacy' for those of us experiencing them in real time and for future generations. Is it possible we can glean a lesson from these two events happening at the same time? Or dare we say even a 'blessing'?
>
> I'd like to share with you, my children, grandchildren and great grandchildren, what I witnessed on those fateful days in May 2020. First, I am writing this and you are reading it

as persons born with white skin. I cannot speak to nor pretend to identify with the deep anger, grief, and frustration of my black and brown brothers and sisters who have endured such ungodly oppression and discrimination at the hands of our society over these past 400 years.

When I first witnessed in horror the fires burning in Minneapolis, destroying the 3rd police precinct, the businesses and homes of innocent people, the looting of stores, I was filled with rage and sadness at the perpetrators of these unlawful acts in the name of protest.

But then something happened to me when I was able to read the message that lay beneath the smoke. The message: "NOW CAN YOU HEAR US?" I realized that those fires were being set by generations of people of color in this country and I remembered why it all suddenly made sense.

I recalled reading African American author James Baldwin's 1963 letter to his young nephew describing growing up black in America. Entitled *The Fire Next Time,* it was written on the 100th anniversary of the Emancipation Proclamation in this country. The book's title was a biblical reference recalling God's warning to Noah's family: that next time destruction would not be by water, but by fire. Those words were prophetic as I watched our city burn.

But I also witnessed something else during those days of looting, rioting, and protesting, something that gave me faith and hope for the future. I saw thousands of my fellow citizens, shoulder to shoulder, arm in arm, from all races and creeds, raising their voices, risking their own lives: calling for justice, a society based on love, not hate, understanding, tolerance, and not prejudice.

At a time when a deadly virus is killing thousands of us because we are not isolating ourselves from each other, maintaining 'social distance' nor wearing face masks, people were willing to risk death to this virus, to come together as one American community and unmask the faces of white privilege and systemic racism.

And so, this is the lesson I want you, my children and grandchildren, to remember. For the majority of citizens on the streets of Minneapolis over those fateful days in May 2020, the desire to undo and address the wrongs and injustices suffered by people of color so that they could truly live emancipated lives in America, was stronger than the desire for their own self-preservation.

There is a word for that . . . 'Love:' The kind of love that James Baldwin was prophetic enough to write to his young nephew over 57 years ago when he argued for a love that 'takes off the mask that we fear we cannot live without and know we cannot live within'.

So here is my lesson to you: sometimes love is louder than silence. Sometimes, it burns.

Love from your Grandpa Bill"

____

____

____

____

____

Here is a poem full of spirit that went viral at the beginning of the pandemic. It was shared by Parker Palmer and Dan Rather among others on social media. Here it is again, "Pandemic" with permission by Lynn Unger, a poet, and UCC minister.

"Pandemic"

"What if you thought of it as the Jews consider the
Sabbath—
the most sacred of times?
Cease from travel.
Cease from buying and selling.
Give up, just for now,
on trying to make the world different than it is.
Sing. Pray. Touch only those to whom you commit your life.
Center down.

And when your body has become still,
reach out with your heart.

Know that we are connected in ways that are terrifying and
beautiful.
(You could hardly deny it now.)
Know that our lives
are in one another's hands.
(Surely, that has come clear.)
Do not reach out your hands.
Reach out your heart.
Reach out your words.
Reach out all the tendrils of compassion that move, invisibly,
where we cannot touch.

Promise this world your love—for better or for worse, in
sickness and in health,
so long as we all shall live."

____

____

____

____

____

One of the first truths COVID-19 taught many of us–or reminded us of–was the importance of family and community. As time slowed to a crawl, we became more aware of who we needed and who needed us. I vividly recall New Year's Eve, 2020–2021, when I heard a knock on my door. I wasn't expecting anyone, I was startled…I opened it…and looked down the hallway….

There were my son and his grown children about six feet away, each masked. They'd come to wish me a good new year. We talked for a few minutes, cautiously and from a safe distance.

When they left, I stood alone in the hallway and shed tears, feeling their love, yet not being able to hug them. Compassionate community nourishes us in different ways, and we all hunger for it.

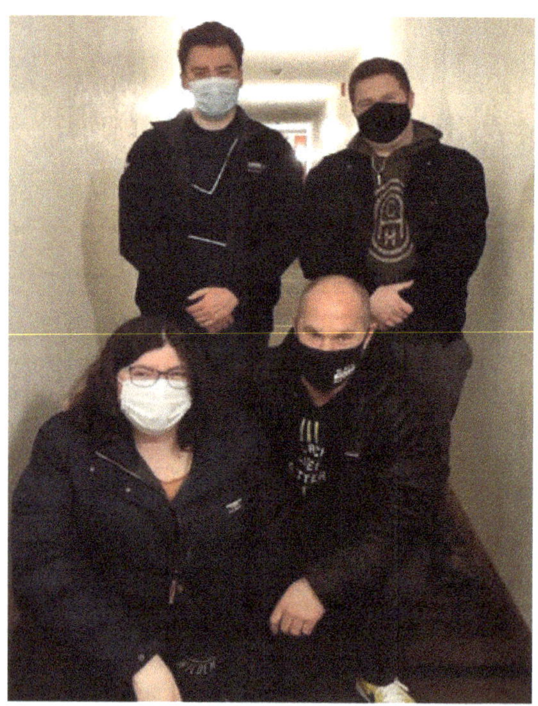

Chapter 2: Change, Loneliness, and Forgetting

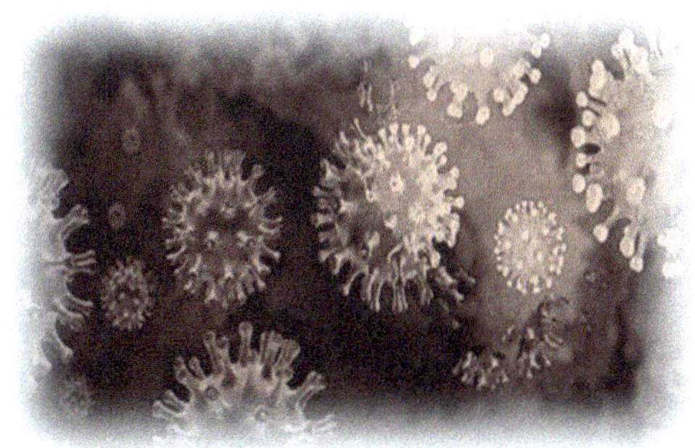

"We cannot forget, because we cannot learn from past mistakes we do not know exist...."

–Ketanji Brown Jackson

Supreme Court Justice

A Zoom Gathering of Legacy Facilitators: Spring, 2020

I initiated a fourth community to gather trained legacy facilitators to offer their insights during the pandemic. My hope was that it would provide a professional community to be a support to them, and to deepen their interest in legacy writing. Each reflection is unique, yet all of them illustrate the grief, resilience, and unexpected grace that emerged during a time of radical uncertainty.

On May 18, 2020, I wrote to the community of trained legacy facilitators as follows:

> "Dear Community of Legacy Facilitators.
>
> This is an invitation to come together for a gathering on Wednesday, May 27, at 7:00 PM, CDT. Here is your Zoom invitation for our gathering:
>
> I invite you to write one or two paragraphs about how the pandemic has affected your life so far, tell a story about it, share what you've learned about yourself in this time. We'll share these when we're together as we deepen our community connection."

The 2020 spring gathering of legacy writing facilitators was planned before I knew where my calling was leading me, but what a gift for the facilitators, for you, for me, and for the next generation to experience these unique legacy reflections.

These writers, like most of us, had never lived through a global pandemic before. What surprised me is how unique each reflection is, and yet, how much they have in common. Their differences…in age, profession, faith, and geography…make their reflections rich and personal. What they have in common is, like all of us, they were navigating unfamiliar territory: fear, isolation, uncertainty, grief, and a longing for connection, meaning, and healing.

Here we are, sixteen little Zoom squares sharing our pain and our learning with each other.

As you read my responses to each of their reflections, consider what feelings and memories they elicit in you and what touches you. Slow down, read and reread these offerings to discover what echoes you hear from the variety of their human experiences, concerns, and styles of expression.

Joan Connor

rebound, reopen, recluse

confusion abounds
communities disengage

from lawmaking governors
we seek leadership -
switching tv channels
peace manifested
leave it buried
the tulip lives from
one hidden bulb

as the essential worker
is to our community
a spirit of sunlight
emanates hope and
beauty beyond –

Rereading the poem I feel the weight of Joan's isolation and I remember my own. In lockdown, silence has its own strange volume. But she closes with hope beginning from the hidden bulb of the tulip. I love that image because it suggests to me spring, rebirth, and bright color, faith in the cycles of change.

Julie Gardner

"After This All Ends"

"When the stay-at-home order came, my 2 1/2-year-old grandson stopped going to his childcare program. I care for him from 8-1:30 every day so his parents can work from home. I was aching for him and wondering what he'd remember from his early years, the pandemic.

"After I wrote this piece, I no longer wonder. He's (we're) having a sweet time. I hope that's what stays with him."

"After this all ends—
What will he remember?

Singing "ABC" and "Happy birthday"
while we wash, wash, wash
"wash away corona, corona, corona."

He says, "Grandpa died" (from the carcinoma)

Does he know people die (from the corona)?
"Ashes, ashes, we all fall down."

No more go to Montessori childcare days.
Mommy and Daddy work from home, have bills to pay.
Grammy comes to play.

There's toys: diggers, dozers and dump trucks,
yellow rubber ducks,
a brand-new doctor's kit.

We read these books-

What are Germs?

At the Construction Site

Cars and Things That Go

'One more, please.'

We can't go play with the neighbors,

at the park, toy store,

on the ferry or anywhere.

.... We paint with fingers,

make handprints on the paper, ...

yogurt-kale-banana-peach popsicles,

baking chocolate chip cookies. ....

... [We paint with water]

Like time, it disappears.

There's lots of kisses, snuggles

tickles, giggles and wiggles

until he squeals, 'Stop! NO! NO!'

I scream silent prayers, No! No!

Please, stop corona.

Let us live.

After this all ends,

What will he remember?"

The end of Julie's tender prose-poem about caring for her grandson took me by surprise : 'screaming silent prayers'. It carried all the despair I feel as an aging woman, not for my own dying as I've already lived the blessing of a full life. I grieve about the damage to my and everyone's children and grandchildren. Her words made visible the sorrow we often carry in silence.

Kathi Gowsell

"Early one morning when all non-essential services in my city and the world had just shut down to limit the spread of COVID-19, I put on my coat and shoes and left the safety of my home for my job at a millwork shop that was deemed essential. Along my commute, there wasn't a soul on the sidewalks nor other cars on the streets.

"It was as though I were the only one in our city risking exposure. At the office, a new sign on the door said, 'STOP.' Only staff were allowed into my workplace, now sterile with the smell of disinfectant and bleach.

"Throughout the day, I washed and sanitized my hands to rawness, tried to focus on my work, and checked the news updates every few minutes.

"Secretly, I wanted to stay home like most others. I wanted to stay in my pajamas until noon, read a book, work on creative projects, clean out my closets and bake chocolate chip banana muffins so I could eat them all myself.

"I felt exhausted by the end of each day yet it felt indulgent to even think of complaining let alone express my fears out loud. I wanted to be grateful for the work as so many around me were losing their jobs. I reminded myself that I was doing my part, helping to keep a little bit of our economy going.

"Two weeks in, I was gaining weight, I was losing sleep, my coping skills, and my retirement dreams. My husband and adult children were working through this time too, some at home, some outside. Each of us was falling apart on some level. We needed to make our mental health a priority and agreed to stretch the rules of isolation to create our three-household 'bubble'. We started to meet weekends, just west of town at the family cabin, a place we could observe social distancing yet be under the same roof. There, we stopped our steady diet of news in favor of games, shared meals and rest. We listened to each other's fears and worries. We took turns caring for each other.

"We counted our blessings. Our gratitude turned our fear into faith that everything would be all right. Slowly, weekend-by-weekend, the pieces of our selves came back together, even though we couldn't hug each other good-bye on Sunday night. Now, I see the whole-hearted family we were before this invisible intruder rocked our world. My home, my workplace and the cabin have become my safe havens.

"I still don't know what the other side of COVID-19 is going to look like but, hugs or no hugs, together we'll get there, the strength of our family bond reinforced."

Kathi's description of the "safe haven" her family created for themselves was an inspiring solution to the isolation of COVID-19. I was tickled by her description of wishing to be at home, doing everything she thought she would do, but especially imagining baking muffins and eating them all herself. That moment of imagined indulgence made her whole reflection so human, so relatable.

____

____

____

____

____

Ann Hass

"Two things stand out for me during this pandemic: 1. I have never been a fearful person and 2. I usually do not feel helpless. I could never have imagined myself fearful to step inside my local grocery store for the first time in six weeks and that a trip in the vegetable aisle could be a "to die for" moment trailing me home. . . .

"Feelings of guilt crept in though after conquering this first fearful trip as the news kept up a continuous flood of stories about long lines at food banks. Was I doing my part by upping my donations to our local food bank? Was there more I could do than send a check and make mounds of face masks for my family, friends, and community? Where is the legacy in that?

"I've had a hard time concentrating and my writing has shut down until recently. This is unusual for me and baffling. Recently, however, I have starting writing pandemic poems and memoir pieces reflecting the impact of this time in our history.

"Finding hope and shedding feelings of helplessness has also been a challenge. I pulled back from an uncommon lethargy and reminded myself that I was checking in with family and friends regularly to see how they were doing and anchoring myself by swapping little bits of hope where we could find it in one another or in the wider world: sharing poems, hiking, nature experiences, and recipes.

"Going on a news diet helped tremendously in tamping down anxiety and reminding me that I did have control over this aspect of my life and that putting the news on hold was not diminishing my role as a good citizen.

"I am proud of my state's response and leadership in Ohio, especially compared to the White House leadership which I have found appalling. My state's response has been uplifting throughout the lockdown and something I can look back on as how our state and community saved lives by our individual and community responses to care for one another.

"Nothing is more uplifting and reassuring than humble leaders relating the facts and if something is unknown, admitting it and trying to find answers and solutions."

I found Ann's piece thoughtful, beginning with her surprise at her personal fear and helplessness. The strength of her recovery from both came from her caring for others, friends, her community, those less fortunate than she, even her pride in her state's response to the emergencies. Her resilience (my word, not hers) grew not from denying fear, but from responding with compassion—from choosing to become part of "we", her communities.

____

____

____

____

____

Bill Marsella

Reflections on Memorial Day May 25, 2020

"Many years ago, when I was still in the military, I was asked by a local American Legion Club to be the keynote speaker for services at the cemetery that day. Dressed in my full uniform, I leaned over the podium and wondered out loud whether families across the country.... took this holiday or the freedom they were enjoying for granted.

"Today we pause to honor and remember our fellow Americans who have given the 'ultimate sacrifice' - their very lives - so that we can enjoy the freedom of living in America That sentiment is still relevant and important today, perhaps even more so, when that freedom has been restricted by the Coronavirus worldwide pandemic.

"The enemy we fight on the battlefield today is not visible but no less lethal than the enemies we fought in all the wars this country has been engaged in since its founding 225 years ago. And the sacrifices being made by our fellow citizens on the front lines of this battle are no less real and courageous. Nearly 100,000 of our fellow citizens have fallen to this virus and countless others have risked their lives on the 'front lines' treating our fallen citizens, risking, and in some cases, losing their own lives in the process.

"Those of us not on the 'front lines' of this war are asked to make our own sacrifices by drastically changing our way of life by living in 'isolation' away from our fellow Americans which is the only weapon that seems to kill this silent enemy. On Memorial Day we pause to reflect on these words "Freedom is 'not' Free"- something tells me these words have never had more meaning than this Memorial Day 2020."

Bill, who served in the military, wrote both to honor those who fought and died for our freedom and to express his appreciation to those 'on the frontlines' risking their health and lives in our war against COVID-19. We don't think of WWII as a pandemic, but the loss of lives in that catastrophe is staggering. The figures I cite here are approximate and from various sources from the internet. In any case, the numbers are shocking: Russian fighters lost are estimated 8.8 to 10.7 million; 10.4 to 13.3 million Russian civilians lost; American fighters lost: 407,300; American civilians lost: 12,100; German military casualties: approximately 5.3 million; German civilians lost are estimated to range from 1.3 to 3.5 million; Jews murdered by Nazis: estimate 6,000,000. It is overwhelming to consider our world buried in grief, so much yet ungrieved, weighing down our planet, like a fog that never fully lifts. When I reflect on WW II, I think of the war as a plague: a global devastation, a pandemic of violence and loss. And now, less than a century later, we face another global sorrow with COVID-19. We are again in a world buried in mourning, aching for expression, and for healing.

____

____

____

____

____

Mary Myers

"The pandemic that is not only sweeping our nation but also the world, has changed life as we have known it and lived it.

"For me, I have been filled with a sense of mourning and heartbreak by the uncertainty, darkness and chaos created by the coronavirus pandemic, feeling very alone at times as the sense of darkness encompasses me.

"Much of what has anchored me and given me a false sense of control in my life, such as freely gathering with family, friends or community, my sense of independence and freedom, my routine, my work in the world that I feel deeply called to do, all have been abruptly halted or, at a minimum, drastically changed. I have felt untethered and unprepared for the volcano of feelings that erupted.

"Initially, I found myself overwhelmed with grief and loss and aimlessly going about my days without focus, routine or intention and without a sense of accomplishment or purpose. Tears were welling up and over-flowing as my fear and deep sadness increased, almost with each breath. The ever-unfolding daily news reports of the pandemic graphically displayed before my eyes, filled my mind - whether awake or asleep - and brought anxiety and physical agitation to my being and broke open my heart and soul. The number of deaths multiplying daily, the crumbling of our social and economic systems and the inherent injustices in our society laid bare by the stories, lives and faces of the suffering, stirred my deep compassion.

"I am a member of that "high-risk" group as a cancer survivor with a bronchial condition. As an "elderly member" of my community, I anticipate my 75th birthday soon. I have survived cancer twice and gone on to thrive and celebrate each day, but my deep fear now is that were I to contract COVID-19, death might accompany this assault on my health and well-being and I might not continue to thrive--I might even die. The fear of becoming seriously ill if I were to contract this virus propelled me into addressing some end-of-life tasks that had been on my mind to complete. More stress."

Mary's deeply honest reflection mirrors I am sure the fears of millions of those high-risk elders and people ill. I was touched by her candid frankness; she "pulled no punches" and I can report as I write in 2025 that she has survived. I was glad to learn that she'd begun writing her end-of-life wishes (and I hope legacy letters to all her loved ones).

____

____

____

____

____

Jeri Okamoto-Tanaka

"I am an introvert by nature and am quite comfortable being home alone (with dogs and sometimes young adult daughters). My work keeps me busy and I don't feel isolated although I do miss being able to see my friends in person. I spend every day with gratitude.

"I was asked to do the sermon for my church's May 24th online worship service to commemorate the 90th anniversary of our historic Japanese American Methodist Church. In preparing, I read, studied and wrote for several weeks. The best part was interviewing two 93-year-old women friends about how they experienced and survived being evacuated from California in 1942 and sent away to the incarceration camps for several years during World War II.

"As with this COVID-19 quarantine, they did not know how long they would be imprisoned - isolated from the outside world. I asked what advice they had for surviving being quarantined. They offered such wisdom, grace, perspective and good humor! Both expressed deep gratitude for being able to be safe at home in such 'luxury' as compared to a barracks in the middle of nowhere: indoor plumbing, good food to eat, television, a phone, freedom. Both shared that their strong faith has kept them connected to a greater power and to one another."

Jeri's interview with two 93-year-old women who'd compared COVID-19 favorably to what they'd suffered in incarceration camps during WWII made me think again about my response to Bill's letter (above) and the similarities of the suffering, loss and grief during WWII and our pandemic today. The women expressed gratitude for what we so casually take for granted: being quarantined free 'at home' not in barracks without indoor plumbing, a phone, television, or good food. Those material privileges were not the case then or now for the poor in our country or around the world. Jeri's reflection reminds us that perspective is a form of wisdom and that gratitude can bridge generations and geography.

Susanna Schuerman

"Her blue satin prom dress hangs in the closet protected by a clear plastic bag. Matching shoes rest on a shelf nearby. Addressed invitations to a graduation, tossed into the dark recess of the desk drawer. Photo boards filled with memories of a seventeen-year old's journey. Like so many high school graduates of 2020, my granddaughter Chloe experienced a graduation she could never have imagined. Instead of an auditorium filled with family and friends, she walked across the stage solo. The school video-taped each student so we could watch it later on cable TV.

"The class of 2020 knows disappointment. They know life can change in an instant. They know phrases like 'social distancing' and 'sheltering in place.' They know how to sew face masks and not hug their grandparents. They know their future is uncertain. Yet, they face life's trials with an admirable willingness to press on.

"Chloe looked at me with a sparkle in her eyes, 'It's all about hope, Grandma. I'm going to college. I am going to be a teacher.'"

As Susanna wrote of the losses and disappointments of young people like her granddaughter I was reminded of one of my own grandsons. In fall 2020, he left home for the first time to attend college on the East Coast. Not long after arriving, he contracted COVID-19 and was placed in strict quarantine–alone in a special dormitory–where his only adventure was to open the door to pick up food left on the floor for him or to go around the corner to the bathroom. He was there in seclusion for ten days, too sick to focus on his school assignments, too alone to feel cared about. He returned home soon after: emotionally battered, depressed, and adrift. It took nearly two years for him to find his bearings and move forward.

Susanna is right! The Class of 2020 knows loss and disappointment. And while their courage matters, so too does our recognition of the wounds they carry.

____

____

____

____

____

Paloma Sulkin

"The day after the Women's Day March, 8th of March 2020 there was a massive manifestation on the main streets of Mexico City, against violence against women.... Next days without any end date - COVID -19!

"I felt, reclined in a hammock, suspended from imaginary hooks above the world, rocked by the time instead of the wind, trying to understand and organize what exactly was happening. The hammock swayed and I saw the world as I knew it, all leveled, in chaos. The hammock swayed back and I saw my little familiar world, threatened by loneliness and fear, but as 'time goes by' -like in the song-my little world started to shine with creativity, Zoom company, pampering by family, and I kept rocking in the hammock, like a pendulum, one side showing the tragedies, the confusion and problems, and swaying back I saw that uncertain times can bring love and reduce fear."

Paloma's powerful vision of swinging in a hammock one way seeing the world in chaos, the other way her familiar world threatened by loneliness and fear. Her vision made me think about my own swing: when I tried to deal with my emptiness and fear by eating and sleeping too much to when I could muster the resilience to rescue a purpose for my life. I created communities and started writing this COVID book in 2023. I stopped oversleeping and overeating and could feel my loneliness and anxiety diminish. I reclaimed the nourishment of communities I shared and what I think of as my personal elder life purpose participating in the larger world. I learned that uncertain times can open unexpected portals: to connection, love, and the deep nourishment of purpose in elderhood.

Joanne Turnbull

"My life has seamlessly crossed the double-yellow line from the in-person to the online world. Each day brings an hour of Zoom contact: A Sunday once-a-month Book Club (skipped by a few zoom haters); each Monday, a half-hour chat with my singing group; Tuesday another hour and a short story discussion; Wednesdays, my online legacy course connects people from Las Cruces, New Mexico with the community left behind in Portland, Maine; Thursdays bring synagogue meetings; and Fridays - blessed Fridays, - my daughters and son meet me at noon.

"Days, even a week, passes before I am forced to put on a bra or shoes. I order a lot of food from the neighborhood restaurant, happy not to cook in the name of keeping a few folks employed. I spend as much time as I can on the back porch enjoying the birds, sky, and mountains before the encroaching heat forces me indoors.

> "The lives of my friends, kids and grandkids have been far more affected. My friend Karen watched her father's Iowa burial on Zoom. Daughter Jenn, a nurse, has been swabbed three times this week, while her sister, Amanda, struggles to find ways to teach drama to high school students. My youngest daughter Megan's job as a television reporter is rewarding once again. Andrew, a stage manager. moved to Philly this fall to be closer to NYC, only to find that his beloved theater world has been replaced by the maws of a state bureaucracy unable to untangle unemployment regulations.
>
> "All five grandkids are bored by the educational system's feeble attempts to teach online and have had all extracurricular activities, including friends, cancelled, making me wonder about kids who spend years in refugee camps."

Joanne's writing about her friend who had to experience her father's funeral online, as did many thousands of others, made me feel again the prevalence and pain of personal loss and grief. Processing grief separated from family complicates the difficulty of grieving and reminds me of Pauline Boss' book about ambiguous loss. Of course, I loved Joanne's honesty about not wearing a bra and going barefoot, a gift for staying home in solitude! Her wondering about the losses of children who spend years in refugee camps brought home the reality of children all over the world losing their parents to COVID-19 without the support we are fortunate to have.

Karen West

"When I was growing up as an only child, my parents didn't give me a lot of physical affection, but as an adult, it seemed to me that more and more people hugged all the time, and I felt rather left out.

"Then when I was a young teacher, one of the male teachers started hugging me. I remember one time when he said "Get ready, Karen. I'm going to hug you." My daughter was also a hugger, so she hugged me, but my son and I were left out. Then a few years ago, I got up all my courage and told my family that I was going to start hugging them, which I did whenever I left their presence. But I couldn't summon up the courage to say, "I love you."

"Because of COVID-19, I didn't see my family for ten weeks. When I finally saw my son, he and his family came to my house to help me in the yard for my Mother's Day present. While they were at my house, they followed the COVID-19 guidelines of not hugging. So, when they were

> leaving and I couldn't hug them, I felt really sad. Then it occurred to me when they were all in the car that I could say, "Because of COVID-19, I know I can't hug you, but I can say "I love you." I almost didn't do it, but happily I did, and it felt so good. Now I just must keep saying it - a gift of the virus."

Karen's courage was palpable in her vulnerable writing, laying bare the pain of her childhood and her risk to make loving physical contact with her children. COVID-19 took away that pleasure and gave her a greater gift: the ability to say the words: 'I love you'.

____

____

____

____

____

Loneliness and Forgetting

Loneliness is another pandemic of our time. It has become more widespread and serious during the pandemic, which advocated quarantining and sheltering-in-place to avoid infection.

Dr. Ruth's final book published after her death in 2024 is titled *The Joy of Connections: 100 Ways to Beat Loneliness and Live a Happier and More Meaningful Life*. She considered herself an expert on loneliness, believing that no one should be ashamed of it. She grew up as a refugee; her parents died in the Holocaust; she was divorced twice and finally widowed. Intolerant of wallowing, her book includes strategies for being more connected to others. She advocated taking risks to get connected, and her favorite metaphor was of turtles: 'A turtle can't hunt for food, bask in the sun, or find a mate if it plays it safe forever; Turtles must take risks in order to live.'

One of the moving poems Laura Hammond submitted for this book is a poignant transition from loneliness to connection, capturing the fear that accompanied her return to life between year one and year two of the pandemic.

Shots and Stuff

"I get my COVID shot next month.

I am excited and terrified.

What will happen when I am free

to leave this apartment,

the one I have been pacing in

for a year?

What will it feel like to ride the bus?

Will I be paranoid? Relieved?

Will I cry at the familiarity and the freedom?

Will I be the only one crying on the bus?

How loud will my first restaurant be?

Have they toned down the music?

Will I be able to avoid eavesdropping?

Where will I go?

Will the library seem like a concert?

Has my concept of quiet changed?

Or space?

Will I ever be the same or has this last year,
and waiting in a small space changed me forever?"

____

____

____

____

____

"When we seek for connection, we restore the world to wholeness.
Our seemingly separate lives become meaningful as we discover
how truly necessary, we are to each other."

– Margaret J. Wheatley

We think of loneliness as being a natural part of being sheltered at home—alone. But Jung suggests a deeper loneliness that explains much of what many of us struggled with in the early years of COVID-19 and still do today. Like about death, we have certain thoughts and feelings we believe separate us from the rest of the human race, cause us to feel shame. This accounts, in part, for the need for this book. Here are Jung's words:

"Loneliness does not come from having no people around,
but from being unable to communicate
the things that seem important to oneself,
or from holding certain views which others find inadmissible."

– Carl Jung

Long before Carl Jung's clarity that being alone differs from loneliness, Rabbi Nachman, born in 1772 in Bratslav (a Ukrainian shtetl) wrote the following prayer:

Grant me the ability to be alone;
may it be my custom to go outdoors each day
among the trees and grass - among all growing things
and there may I be alone, and enter into prayer,
to talk with the One to whom I belong.

May I express there everything in my heart,
and may all the foliage of the field -
all grasses, trees, and plants -
awake at my coming,
to send the powers of their life into the words of my prayer
so that my prayer and speech are made whole

through the life and spirit of all growing things,
which are made as one by their transcendent Source.

May I then pour out the words of my heart
before your Presence like water, O God,
and lift up my hands to You in worship,
on my behalf, and that of my children.

In fall of 2024 I watched a fascinating documentary about The Tenement Immigration Museum on the lower east side of Manhattan, housed in two mid-1800s buildings on the corner of Orchard and Delancey Streets. You might wonder how that's relevant to a legacy writing book focused on Covid-19.

Often whole families visit the museum together and respond not only by learning about the families who lived there over decades and centuries, communities of Russian Jews, Italians, Puerto Ricans, and Chinese, but then they begin to tell stories previously unknown about their own families and deepen their own family connections.

The documentary explained how visitors tapered to zero during the pandemic, and the museum, dependent on visitors' fees, had scrambled just to remain open. Aware of restaurants and shops closing for want of customers during Covid-19, I'd never considered the cultural and community losses and the importance of museums and libraries, concert halls and movie theaters, and the financial struggles they and their personnel experienced as well as the cultural losses their patrons faced during the pandemic.

In 2023, US Surgeon General Vivek H. Murphy M.D. wrote "an advisory" of 82 pages, titled "Our Epidemic of Loneliness and Isolation" calling out the main causes of social disconnection as Covid and technology. He estimated that a lack of social connection affects more Americans than diabetes or obesity, and observed results of increased health risks: physical, emotional and mental. He suggested "Six Pillars" to advance social connection, the 6th being to "cultivate a Culture of Connection".

From my reading and psychotherapeutic background, I learned that loneliness is less about being physically alone, but instead feeling "emotionally al one "; not being cared for or about; fe eling like an outsider or believing oneself unw orthy of a community, but . . .

". . . . disasters thrust people back into a more ancient, organic way of relating. Disasters create a 'community of sufferers' that allows individuals to experience an immensely reassuring connection to others. As people come together to face an existential threat . . . differences are temporarily erased ...."

– Charles Fritz, in *Tribe,* by Sebastian Junger, 2016

In March of 2023, Richard Sima wrote an article about the science of forgetting for *The Washington Post.* He with other scientists explained how our brains tend mainly to recall personal experiences. Unless we were personally affected: having lost a loved one, having dealt with symptoms of long Covid, or having been burned out by dealing with daily loss in a health care setting, many details fade over time. Our brains have limitations, which may be emotionally protective, and newer events bombard our brains daily.

Another explanation for forgetting is that for many people COVID -19 was a very unpleasant time. When we focus on "wanting to get on with life" or "getting back to normal", our memories become counterproductive.

"Francis Weller, author of *The Wild Edge of Sorrow*, declared his view of the serious consequences of our forgetting:

> "I wrote this book to address the two primary sins of Western civilization: amnesia and anesthesia—we forget and we go numb. These two sins account for an amazing range of sorrows."

____

____

____

____

____

I don't believe anyone could have expressed the importance of remembering COVID-19 and the dangers of us forgetting it better than Elliot Kirschner did in his 2024 powerful post "The Trauma of Covid" in his newsletter, "Through the Fog", on *Substack*. He wrote:

"… the damage I know lurks in crevices of ourselves and our communities in ways many of us are oblivious to or wish to ignore." With his gracious permission I share his post with you in full.

> "…I fear there is something about seeing the word COVID-19 in a headline or title that creates a deep ambivalence about whether one wants to engage. I often feel it as well.
>
> "I know it is important. I know it was devastating. I know it is still with us. I know it changed our world in profound ways. I know it is one of the most important stories of our time, inextricably wrapped up in other narratives around our democracy, our economy, our mental and physical health, the

education of our children, the vibrancy of our cities, our relationship with the rest of the world, and on and on.

"But there is something about this accumulated trauma that drives at least my survival instincts to want to move on. How crisp are your memories of disinfecting groceries, wondering when or if you would ever travel or gather in large groups again, the terror of being near someone who just coughed?

"When I summon these snapshots, I remember those days of isolation and unknowing. But it is as if they exist in their own photo album, profoundly different from memories before and since.

"As I spent the last few days walking around New York City — the epicenter of death and suffering when the virus hit four years ago — I am struck by how, on the surface, you would basically never know it.

"The restaurants are full. The streets are crowded. There is rarely a mask in sight.

"And yet, the damage I know lurks in crevices of ourselves and our communities in ways many of us are oblivious to or wish to ignore.

"Not everyone has that luxury.

"First and foremost, I know that many families were torn apart by the disease that claimed over one million deaths in the United States alone. There are empty seats at the dinner table, missing loved ones at family reunions, and friends who will never return a phone call again. My heart aches for all of them. Countless more still suffer the effects of long COVID-19. Lives, often of those still quite young, are forever altered. And then there are all of the unknowns about how Covid will affect our long-term health. It will take decades of study to determine that cost.

"If the physical pain and suffering were the limits of the disease, it would still deserve far more attention than it gets, but that is sadly only the beginning. I look at my children and wonder how this timespan when the world stopped shaped their sense of self and their futures. I know we are relatively fortunate. Many children will never catch up from the years they lost away from school and socializing with others.

"I look at my beloved city of San Francisco. It is still early in its recovery act, but it will be a profoundly different place because of the societal disruptions from COVID-19. I think about my job as a science communicator and bemoan how cynical political actors shattered critical bonds of trust between scientists and the public. I think about how, far too often, we bury the terrible news of the past rather than learn from it.

"I lived in New York after 9/11, and I think about how that horrific act is memorialized in the city and the nation. How we vow never to forget. And then I think of the scale of destruction from COVID-19 and how we are eager to move on, except for all those who cannot. In some ways, it reminds me of the war in Iraq that followed the terrorist attacks; it was a burden borne for years by only a tiny percentage of the population, while the rest of us could afford to skip past the headlines for that tragedy as well.

"Americans are good at moving forward. Something in our national character, emotional makeup, and basic human instincts propel us to look at the road ahead and not in the rearview mirror. It is a source of strength and resilience, to a point. We have had one of the best recoveries from COVID-19 of any nation.

"But there is also something that is being lost. We owe it to those who died from the disease and their friends and loved ones not to forget. We need to study our myriad mistakes — at the level of government, public health, individuals and so much more. We need to make sure we avoid them in the future. We need to confront the disunity the disease exacerbated.

"I hope that, with time, the passions that tragically politicized this pandemic and resulting public health catastrophe will subside. On the fourth anniversary of COVID-19 being declared a national emergency, we can find a path to more profound healing.

"I know there are a lot of challenges facing our nation, but I don't want to discount the profound effects of this horrible disease and what it wrought.

"It might not seem a priority, but I join those calling for a national COVID-19 memorial in Washington. On the National Mall.

"Often, the things we most want to ignore and forget are precisely what we most need to remember."

The following wise and loving reflection was written by Michelle Riddell, a Michigan mother, to her daughter, first published on a Facebook page labelled *Love What Matters*. Its title: "You Will Want to Remember This".

"Maybe not next year or the year after, but someday, when the shock and horror wear off, when we are sitting next to each other at say, a baby shower or a band concert, so close that my sleeve brushes yours, and we exchange a look that recalls these strange days—you will want to.

"You will want to remember how it felt to wake up in the morning, how it took a moment for the cloud of sleep to lift, and then another for the cloud of day to settle, and how you would ask yourself, 'What did I do yesterday? Did I shower? Did it rain?'

"You will want to remember how you passed the time, how you became mesmerized by colorful cardboard shapes and lettered tiles and playing cards, how you drifted off in thought, mid-turn, worrying about the kids at school.

"You will want to remember how at last, when you had all the time in the world to read, you couldn't tame your mind beyond a sentence.

"Maybe, like me, you lost yourself in a closet or a drawer, emerging hours later, aimlessly clutching saved baby clothes and key chains bought on vacation.

"Maybe, like me, you felt guilt and relief about being healthy, safe, spared.

"Maybe, like me, you cried watching a music video, a dreamy, haunting rendition of 'A Day in the Life', so harrowingly beautiful it hurt.

"You will want to remember how, in this time, some people turned inward, some to nature, some to humor, some to God.

"How, when we all felt helpless, some made bread, others art.

"Some made masks.

"Others wore them.

"How phrases like 'virus shedding' and 'social distancing' became part of our vernacular, how we ran out of ways to say 'unprecedented.'

"How we kept running tallies of our infected and our dead.

"How you stopped caring, or started caring, or wished you'd been a better daughter.

"You will want to remember how you changed, how you went from the rigid enforcer to letting your kids eat cake in their bedrooms. How you learned to wait. How you learned what mattered.

"Maybe you made a schedule.

"Maybe you upheld the bedtime routine.

"Maybe you called your mom at midnight just to hear her sigh and tell you to get some sleep.

"You need to remember this. I want you to remember this, because years from now, a lifetime from now, when we're leaving somewhere, saying goodbye, when I'm hugging you tight and tighter still, and we both laugh, and yet I don't let go–you will know why."

This 2024 poignant poem "A Pandemic Summer" needs no explanation: written by Patsy Glista, after the loss of her husband, and shared with her permission.

"We did not know, you and I

That summer we spent

Just the two of us in our garage porch

No family gatherings — No weekend getaways
Just you and I alone in our porch

You watched the many walkers strolling by

And read car literature — a new car to find us

I colored and cross-stitched

Filling the days

Root-beer floats at home

Instead of ice cream treat rides

Evenings we sat on the patio out back

Watching robins scurry for worms

And the neighbor's resident groundhog

Our only outing, the grocery store

Masks secured, you checking the list,

Gloves on my hands

We were determined to stay well

We did not know, you and I,

That summer would be our last

You would never see summer again

And those days would become

My most precious memories"

____

____

____

____

____

As the pandemic's grip loosened, the world rushed toward normalcy, eager to forget, to move on. But forgetting is a kind of silence. And silence has a cost. Beneath the masks, beneath the headlines, beneath even the visible losses, grief lingered… unspoken. What remains unexpressed does not vanish. It sinks like a stone in water, into our bodies, into generations of family, into the culture.

The grief of COVID-19, like the griefs of wars, genocides, and plagues before it, will not stay quiet forever. In Chapter 3, we'll explore the grief we couldn't express, the secrets we held, how silence shapes what is passed down to future generations, and ask what it means to tell the truth of our pain.

Chapter 3: Unexpressed Grief

– the Secrets of COVID-19 –

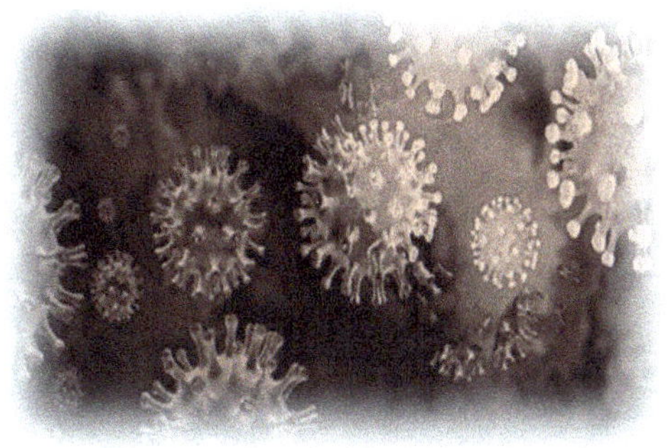

"The human soul doesn't want to be advised or fixed or saved. It simply wants to be witnessed — to be seen, heard, and companioned exactly as it is."

– Parker J. Palmer

Susan Griffin's insights in *A Chorus of Stones: The Private Life of War* helped me understand the danger of keeping COVID-19 secrets. It also reminded me of the costs of silence passed down from first- to second-generation Holocaust survivors. Rutha Rosen's poem, "COVID–Three Weeks In" made a connection with the two "pandemics".

COVID- Three Weeks In

"Colleagues and clients are sick and dying
I am in a state of high anxiety
I imagine how it must have been for Jews
during the 2nd World War, secluded in their homes
in degrees of denial.

We live in the most surreal of circumstances
hidden by masks, running through a minefield
for a loaf of bread.

Darwin said that species adapted to their circumstances
to survive, is this what is happening here?

Will the fittest survive?

Theories swamp the internet.

A scientist working on a theory that a virus prevalent in bats

may have been transmitted to humans

has disappeared, everything is vague.

New York City has been hit so hard

everyone knows someone who is sick or dying or dead

and around the world each one is thinking

will I be next!"

____

____

____

____

____

According to research by Ronnie Dunetz in his 2023 unpublished dissertation, Holocaust survivors kept silent about their experiences for many reasons; nearly all of which mirror the silence surrounding pandemic experience.

Some could not speak of it. The trauma was too horrific.

Some tried to bury their memories in order to survive.

Some felt they couldn't live with the truth and just tried to "be happy."

Some bore deep survivor guilt, especially about the actions they took to stay alive.

Some wanted to distance themselves from their past and project strength instead of vulnerability.

Some were silenced by others, people who didn't want to listen or wouldn't believe them.

Many Holocaust survivors believed they were protecting their children by keeping silent. But their children, second-generation survivors, often suffered mental and emotional harm as a result. Many felt profound loneliness during COVID-19 without understanding why. But by keeping silent, yet another opportunity was lost. The same secrets, the same stones, get handed down to the third and fourth generations.

This illustrates an important truth: **legacy is passed down whether it is spoken or not.** If we do not give voice to our individual and communal experiences during the COVID-19 pandemic, the harm of silence will echo forward.

"... a nameless grief now named hence lifted

when we hear any secret revealed...."

– Susan Griffin

These three words...**shame, stigma and fear...**kept Holocaust survivors silent. Perhaps they help explain why so many COVID-19 survivors have kept silent too:

- Shame that we failed our dying loved ones.
- Stigma for hoarding or breaking rules about wearing masks or social distancing .
- Fear of dying.

Unlike past generations, we are no longer steeped in silence. We live in an age of speech, documenting everything, from the important to the inane, on every digital platform imaginable. But that isn't the same as **expression**. Social media may share statistics, news, and even rage, but little is known about the **true human cost** of the pandemic. Few opportunities exist to give voice to secret sadness or to grieve collectively.

"If losses are not dealt with, the trauma of unresolved
grief can be passed down from generation to generation.
We see this transmission today of traumatizing losses,
incurred centuries ago—the genocide of Native

Americans, the injustice and pain of slavery, the horrors of the Holocaust, plus endless wars and genocides never officially acknowledged and still not resolved."

- Pauline Boss
author of *Ambiguous Loss*

Ironically, the silence in grieving families today echoes that of families who lost loved ones during the 1918 Spanish Flu. How rare it is still to say our goodbyes, to recount our stories, to express our love and grief, to share what we've learned from our experiences of loss, to leave a meaningful legacy for future generations.

We're already "forgetting" COVID-19. Many believe it's over and have moved on. In May 2023, the World Health Organization officially declared: "The pandemic is over."

"The past is not dead, it's not even past."

–William Faulkner, *Requiem for a Nun*

But *The Washington Post* in August of the same year published this correction: "The coronavirus has not disappeared. With the advent of successful vaccinations and better social management, however, it has waned."

In his darkly satirical self–published 2025 book *Forbidden History: Volume 3: Plagues, Prophets, and People Who Should Not Have Been in Charge,* Justin Gross wrote:

> "It wasn't until the 1990s, when new scholarship emerged that the true scope of the Spanish Flu's devastation became widely known. And even now, it remains one of the least publicly commemorated catastrophes in human history, despite killing more people in a single year than the entire Holocaust. So, what did we learn? Not much.
>
> "We learned that governments do lie to preserve the illusion of control. That nationalism makes pandemics worse. That propaganda kills. That racism is always waiting to be weaponized. . . . That science matters—but only if you listen to it. And we learned that pandemics don't just kill bodies; they erode institutions, expose hypocrisy, and leave wounds that fester in silence for generations.
>
> "The Spanish Flu wasn't just a tragedy: it was a warning. And like all good historical warnings, it was ignored the moment the caskets stopped overflowing. No one restructured global health systems. No one prioritized virology. No one said, 'Let's make sure this never happens again.' They said, 'Well, that was awful,' and moved on. Until 2020. Because when COVID-19 exploded onto the scene, the ghost of the Spanish Flu rose with it. Same

panic. Same lies. Same masks, same protests, same morons screaming about liberty....

"It was like watching a remake of a film no one remembered seeing....The Spanish Flu taught us that ignoring a virus doesn't make it disappear. That early action saves lives. That public trust is the difference between manageable and massacre. But when COVID hit, most governments fell back into the same cowardly instincts: delay, deny, deflect.

"The difference now was that information spread faster than the virus, and so did misinformation. In 1918, your neighbor might pass you a rumor. In 2020, your uncle reposted Russian disinformation.... The Spanish Flu was a test. We failed it. Then we forgot it. And then we got tested again a century later. If there's any lesson worth dragging out of that graveyard .... it's that forgetting is the most dangerous thing we can do.

"Pandemics are not rare. They are part of the human condition. The real question is not 'Will another one come?' but 'Who will be in charge when it does?' And if the answer is 'a man who thinks bleach is a cure,' we're already coughing in the wrong direction. Spanish Flu showed us that disease is biological, but disaster is political. That nature starts the fire, but humans pour the gasoline. That leadership matters more than luck and lies kill more efficiently than germs."

According to *Newsweek,* citing CDC data from December 2024, more than **1.21 million Americans** died of COVID-19. Globally – over **7 million**. Many died alone, without the opportunity to speak final words, to receive comfort, to hold or hug those of us left behind, to give or receive blessings, or to pass on wisdom.

Multiply that loss by the number of their family members, friends, and communities, and you get a staggering number of people who now carry unspoken grief.

> "It is a great truth that says that the worst blind person
> is the one who did not want to see."
>
> – Jose Saramago in *Blindness*

Dr. Atul Gawande, assistant administrator for global health at USAID wrote in *The New York Times* (March 2023): Total deaths globally jumped by 13 percent in the first two years of the pandemic, pushing life spans and human development backwards for the first time since World War II.

As health systems buckled under the weight of COVID-19 care, routine services were suspended. Burned out, many healthcare workers left their professions completely. Immunizations dropped. Cancer screenings lapsed. Mental health support disappeared when we needed it most.

How confusing! So—is it over or not?

Either way, we are left with a secondary pandemic:

- To speak or stay silent,
- To feel, or to numb
- To remember or forget?
- Whether to welcome our grief or proceed like robots.

As a culture, we seem intent on forgetting. We long to "get back to normal." But what if forgetting is the very thing we cannot afford?

George Wylesol writing in *The Washington Post* (March 13, 2023), explored "The Science of Forgetting: Why We're Already Losing Our Pandemic Memories."

> "As a society, many people don't want to hold on to their pandemic memories." And yet he wrote that COVID-19 will be part of our life stories as is 9/11 the terror attack that took down the Twin Towers in New York City.
>
> "It would be easier to understand forgetting about the pain, losses, and change of COVID-19 if it really had disappeared. But 2,000 Americans were still dying weekly in 2023, and we'd already begun to pretend the pandemic never happened. "

____

____

____

____

____

In his 1923 "short story", "The Rats in the Walls", H.P. Lovecraft wrote:

> "Ultimate horror often paralyzes memory
> in a merciful way."

AARP's Bulletin that focuses on people over 50 hadn't forgotten in September 2024. As I complete my final edit in January 2026, the CDC and other reputable sources say that the new Covid variant is rising in the US. Due to our political situation, unless one is older than 65, the vaccine is difficult to procure and will be costly for a large per centage of our population.

But here is the core of my fear: **if we forget, we lose the very lesson the pandemic was trying to teach us... to grieve.**

Francis Weller, in *The Wild Edge of Sorrow: Rituals of Renewal and the Sacred Work of Grief (2015)*, wrote:

> "When grief remains unexpressed, however, it hardens, becomes as solid as a stone. We, in turn, become rigid..... Without intimacy with grief, our capacity to be with any other emotion or experience in our life is greatly compromised.... grief has always been communal and illustrates how we need the healing touch of others, an atmosphere of compassion, and the comfort of ritual ... to fully metabolize our grief."

___

___

___

___

___

When we hide our grief, whether for those we've lost, the life we once knew, or the fear we carry, **it echoes through the generations**.

Anne K. Gross, in her book *The Polio Journals* wrote, trying to "make sense of the legacy of my mother's illness and the price all of us paid for not speaking the truth." She described growing up in a family bound by silence. Reading her mother's journals decades later helped her realize the unspoken toll, how even illnesses like polio ripple forward in time, shaping not just lives, but legacies.

In *The New York Times*, David Wallace-Wells wrote in December 2023:

"The pandemic not only killed more than a million Americans
but also threw much of daily life and
public confidence into disarray....
scarring our perceptions of this country,
its capacities, and its future."

All that we've hidden, forgotten, or numbed (whether from exhaustion or pain) still lives within us. It will continue to shape the next generation unless we speak.

If we learned anything from this pandemic: about ourselves, about each other, about loneliness, fear, or failure, we owe it to the future to express it.

To write. To speak. To remember.

We cannot rewrite the past, but we can refuse to erase it. Our silence will not protect us, nor will it protect those who come after us.

We've unearthed the silence, named the secrets, and felt the weight of unspoken sorrow. Now, we enter the terrain of grief itself, where death cracks us open, where mourning teaches us, and where resilience, like a strong green shoot, finds light through the cracks.

____

____

____

____

____

As we turn from the hidden sorrows of the pandemic (those unspoken, unnamed, and long-silenced) we move into one of the most enduring silences of all: death itself. If grief was once a secret we carried, death remains the deepest mystery. In the chapter ahead, we open that silence gently, truthfully, and with love. To write of death is not to lose hope, but to affirm the sacredness of life and the enduring power of legacy.

Chapter 4: Death, Grief, and Resilience

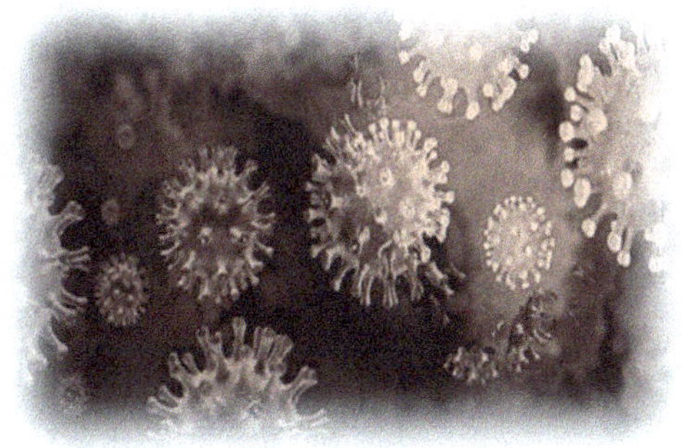

"Grief and resilience live together"

– Michelle Obama, *Becoming*

About Death

It was 1959 when Kubler-*Ross' On Death and Dying* was written. Yet 65 years later death remains a secret...an unmentionable subject at most dinner tables, even off-limits in serious discussions to plan our futures. In legacy writing, I have observed that when we stay silent about aging, dying, and death, that silence becomes the legacy we leave our children and the generations that follow. Conversely, when we speak about death as a natural part of life, as its end, or perhaps its beginning, we pass down a more open, honest legacy.

> I remember an afternoon some years ago - a sunny summer Sunday - when my son and his four children accompanied me to the cemetery to choose my plot. There was no one else there. The kids, ages three to eight, frolicked among the headstones. Only the older two understood, even a little, what we were doing.
>
> The oldest, Mitch, asked me whether I would put a bench by my grave so he could come and read to me as I'd read to him. I teared up as I pointed out a nearby grave with a stone bench that also served as a headstone. We agreed it would be perfect. Then his sister Lily began to cry ... she wanted a bench too. I pointed to a square stone flowerpot, and asked if she would come and tend its flowers if I had one? Her eyes sparkled as she agreed, then she went off to play with her brothers among the graves.

Though not a monumental (no pun intended) experience, I felt glad and proud that part of my legacy to them would be this early and gentle normalization of death and burial. Perhaps it would stay with them as they matured, and eventually, when they joined others in burying me.

____

____

____

____

____

In 2021, Erin Leib Smokler, author of *Torah in a Time of Plague*, wrote about the relationship of the plague of COVID-19 and death.

> "The experience of almost, the fragility of things, during the pandemic we became cognizant that we all stand on the cusp of death at every moment ....One response is shock, dizziness, and even nausea, awareness of randomness, consciousness that the whiplash, being lost in the world that is highlighted by the catastrophe....we experience always that we live with that uncertainty... that we could be here one day and not the next, and we have dealt with that existential awareness of the pandemic. Coming to terms with the pandemic is but a hair's breadth of reckoning with death."

In her book, *Pandemic 1918: Eyewitness Accounts from the Greatest Medical Holocaust in Modern History*, Catharine Arnold included this account:

"One morning a young woman arrived at Brockton Hospital suffering from Spanish flu. Her lungs were already full of blood, and she was seven months pregnant. 'The baby was born prematurely and died at birth, but I did not dare tell the mother it had died,' recalled her nurse. She kept begging me to see her baby… I assured her that he was fine and beautiful and she would hold him as soon as she was stronger. She had such a lovely look on her face as she talked about her son, and how happy her husband would be. It was an effort for her to talk as her lungs were filling….She died late that afternoon. I put the baby into her arms and fixed them so that they seemed only to be sleeping. And so, the husband saw them when he came."

Are we still as fearful about acknowledging death as we were during and after the flu epidemic of 1918? Have we not yet broken through the taboo of earlier decades and centuries? Do we still believe that to speak of death is somehow dangerous? Are we still suspicious or superstitious that speaking about death may somehow hasten our own?

Have we been conditioned to believe that grief should be brief—that we should "get over it" and "get back to normal" quickly? Or are we simply so overwhelmed by the changes faced in COVID-19 that we've become paralyzed: unable to feel, think, or act?

Are we so encased in our privilege that we imagine ourselves immune to change, believing that denial can shield us from suffering? Are our feelings so dulled, frozen, or immobilized that we cannot grieve?

Are we so misinformed that we see no value in science, research, or preparation for the next pandemic which will surely come? Is there something(s) specific we're afraid to face? Has Covid become so politicized that we hesitate to speak of it at all?

What are the unintended consequences of our silence and inaction, for ourselves and for generations to come? When will we recognize that we are shaped by our time just as we are by our past, and that both past and present shape our future and the future of those we love?

Although these are only questions, writer James Thurber once said:

"It's better to know
some of the questions
than all of the
answers."

What we know about Grief

When I first read Pauline Boss's book, *Ambiguous Loss: Learning to Live with Unresolved Grief* in 2000, I began to understand personally what "ambiguous loss" meant. It manifests in two ways: when we grieve those who are physically present but psychologically absent, and when, as during COVID-19, we grieve those who are physically gone but psychologically present. Many people had no chance to be with their loved ones at the end… no bodies to pray over or bury, and in some cases, no tangible proof of death. These people continue to grieve their losses and may continue to have hope that one day their loved ones will return.

Minx Boren, founder of *BalancePoint Newsletters*, www.coachminx.com, expresses the pain of ambiguous loss in her untitled poem ©Minx Boren. She articulates what it meant to her to be separated during the pandemic, unable to touch those she loved. She wrote in specific detail how we grieve someone who is here but not here. I share her poem with her permission:

"We are all so sadly out of touch

even though we are not out of reach

thanks to technology

that leaps across physical miles

but without getting physical with one another

and wrapping our arms around

we are stuck in a terrible state

of huglessness

bracing ourselves against the embrace

that never comes

our touchy-feely nature

is thwarted again and again

as we keep our distances

settling for fist bumps

and elbow kisses

how very unsettling

this lack of sensory connection

taking its toll on our

primal yearning to be greeted and held

and comforted up close

and personally"

Two decades after her first book, Boss returned to these themes in *The Myth of Closure: Ambiguous Loss in a Time of Pandemic and Change.* She reaffirmed that grief does not end, but resilience can grow. Resilience can provide hope and the strength to live our lives in a way that is stronger, more positive.

> "we live with our grief all of our lives, whether expressed or not....when ambiguous losses can't be prevented, it is resilience, not closure, that provides us with new hope and the strength to live life in a new way.....resilience means increasing our tolerance for ambiguity ....letting go of the idea of closure and instead, finding meaning in our losses; thinking both/and about the positive and negative, increasing our tolerance for ambiguity."
>
> – Pauline Boss

Boss also clarified that Elisabeth Kübler-Ross's five stages of grief were never meant to suggest that we would move through them neatly to "closure." Even Kübler-Ross came to agree that life continues with grief, not beyond it. We grow into resilience through remembering and grieving. But the event and its accompanying grief are the necessary ingredients to develop resilience.

"death ends a life not a relationship"

– Mitch Albom, *Tuesdays with Morrie*

Albom's quote brings to mind a legacy workshop I led years ago in Cleveland. It was just before the Jewish High Holy Days, and I'd invited participants to write legacy letters of amends or forgiveness.

> Afterward, a young woman approached me and said quietly, "I think I did it wrong." I explained there was no right or wrong in legacy writing and interpreted her comment as wanting to tell me what she'd written. I invited her to communicate her concerns. She said succinctly, "I wrote to my dad." I explained that we can write to those before us, after us, and among us. Then she added, "But my father is dead."
>
> I said, "What makes you think the relationship ends because you're here and he's not?" She frowned and walked away. But

before leaving, she turned and said, "Thank you. I couldn't have done it while he was alive."

Mary Shelley asked "Why live?" after the deaths of her three children and husband Percy. In her 1826 novel *The Last Man*, she tried to answer her own question. The novel, set in the midst of a world pandemic, imagines the last man alive in 2099. He questions the meaning of human life, writing down all that has happened to humanity. Writing about nature, he glimpses meaning.

> "Winter passed away; and spring, led by the months, awakened life in all nature. The forest was dressed in green; the young calves frisked on the new-sprung grass; the wind-winged shadows of light clouds sped over the green cornfields .... and the young green of the trees lay in gentle relief along the clear horizon .... There is but one solution to the intricate riddle of life; to improve ourselves and contribute to the happiness of others."

Observing the resilience of nature, Shelley's protagonist regains his faith not only in survival but in the beauty and value of life as he approaches an understanding of nature's resilience.

"There will be no closure on this hellish time.

It will leave its mark on all of us, and like the great depression

and World War II, we shape an entire Generation."

– Pauline Boss

Angelina Aller, a creative professional, shared her personal story: the shock of a "six-week lockdown" that became a life change; the move to a new home; a pandemic pregnancy; the grief of losing her father; and the lingering anxiety. Her story helps us remember the unrecorded, unmeasured weight many women bore during COVID.

> "Six weeks?! That timeline rushed through my head. I was sitting at my desk at our corporate headquarters looking through the few items I needed to pack up. I had just gotten back from a work trip and we were told that we should be prepared to work from home.
>
> "The Covid-19 virus had spread far enough into the United States that even large corporations were taking actions to keep communities safe. Working from home wasn't completely foreign to me. Our company allowed us to work from home when needed.

"I work in a creative field and our desk spaces were open and 'collaborative'. What that meant was our whole lives were shared. It was not uncommon to overhear conversations of another person's activities: doctor appointments, car troubles, engagements, bad dates or calls from daycare or schools. Over the ten years I'd worked at this corporate office, I had been through some big life milestones: dating, marriage, and having my first child.

"My village of friends were my co-workers. I had met some of my closest friends at work, and we had shared many experiences because we spent more than 40+ hours together five days a week. Six weeks at home was going to be a long time without those friends. Little did I know that those six weeks would turn into a new way of working and living for me and my family.

"In May of 2020, my husband, our 3-year-old son, and I moved into our first home in a quaint neighborhood not far from our first condominium home. In the height of the Covid pandemic, our move was quiet. We met neighbors from afar on the streets outside as we went for walks or played in the front yard. Since human connections were so rare those days, even a wave through a front window felt warming and brought a sense of comfort.

"Our daily mailman introduced himself as "King" Richard and has never told my kids the same joke twice. Our garbage man Kyle would beep the horn twice and wave to our kids every

Thursday morning. We met all the families on our street and shared our Covid experiences together.

"Raising little kids during the pandemic was a challenge none of us thought we would have to experience. Having other families around helped to ease the stress, offered a sense of community and gave me the village I no longer had with my coworkers. Routines changed and Covid became part of everyday life, at least for a while. Our home has a different meaning now, as it's a permanent office for me. It allowed me to be more present with my children, taught me how to draw boundaries between work and home life, and it's my village of mothers and friends.

"In May of 2021, we had our second child, a pandemic baby. It was an isolating pregnancy. My husband was not allowed to accompany me to my prenatal doctor appointments and I had to share the news with my family at an outdoor patio party with our chairs six feet apart. I hardly left the house because pregnancy labeled me an individual at 'high risk'. It was too early in the pandemic to know how Covid would affect babies in the womb. I stayed home, did prenatal yoga in my living room, and like so many others, learned to bake bread.

"I took my first Covid shot when I was 36 weeks pregnant, the day the FDA announced it was safe for expectant mothers. It was scary and a relief at the same time. I prayed I was doing the right thing for my baby, and administering the vaccine encouraged me. I was trusting science and facts to keep me and my baby safe. What I did not realize at the time, was that going through pregnancy during the pandemic would cause me anxiety for years after my baby was born. I was so concerned with keeping myself and my babies safe that I developed anxiety whenever anyone got even minor symptoms of a cold. A runny nose, Covid test. An extra sneeze, Covid test. Dry throat, Covid test. Trying to keep the virus away from my family was my first priority at all times.

"My father lived in a nursing home during the pandemic. He'd moved there in 2017 suffering advanced multiple sclerosis. He chose not to get the vaccine because it would exacerbate his MS symptoms. He had been paralyzed from the waist down for some time, so any delay of his parting from this earth was not something he was interested in.

"He caught the Covid virus at the beginning of February 2022; one midnight I got a call that he had taken a turn for the worse. I picked up my mom and we went to the hospital. Sitting in the ER with him, watching him breathe into an oxygen mask, is an image that will never leave my memory. Because of my anxiety, I couldn't even bring myself to touch him. I stood next to him, hoping he would recognize me through the large K95 hospital grade mask, and told him that I loved him.

"I watched them wheel him into a room in the Covid Unit and I watched him from the hallway, never entering the room. My dad was made comfortable, and after the chaplain visited, Dad slowly left us. I did not hug him, did not hold his hand, nor thank him for making me his favorite daughter. It's my life's biggest regret."

"The world breaks everyone,
afterward many are strong at the broken places."

–Ernest Hemingway

Susan Eastman Tilsch, a friend who lost her 17-year-old son when he took his own life, shared her insight that speaks to the heart of legacy work: honoring grief while learning the resilience born of forgiveness and freedom.

"I once came across the words 'honest in our pain' and they spoke to me. I think sometimes people run from the pain. They don't want to feel it, but I believe it is in knowing and exploring that pain and the loss, there can be growth, memories and freedom.

"Interestingly, it took me many years to see and to understand that 'freedom' can come with deep, honest, and painful grieving. It took more losses and more years before I grasped that I didn't have to be captive to the loss forever. There was clearly a possibility to feel more than just pain, guilt or regrets, and most importantly the freedom to experience more of life.

"I didn't have to hurt forever to keep these precious people alive within me.

"I remember a moment of clarity hearing a mother who'd lost a teenager tell her dream of him visiting her. She described her joy and their hugs. He asked her, 'Mom, what have you been doing with your life in these years since I've been gone?' She was silent.... Then she said, 'Grieving you.' When I heard her story, I realized I didn't want to meet my Christopher without having a real answer of what I've done with my life since he left!

"I stayed very busy, but then COVID hit and changed our lives. The COVID days were not easy ones. I was restless and uncomfortable but very gradually without knowing it, I was going deeper. Gone were the outside diversions, the activities and the trips. I was now face to face with my thoughts, my loss and the walls of my townhouse.

"There was one other completely unexpected discovery; I realized I had to learn to forgive myself: to forgive my mistakes, my missteps. Never before had I seen forgiveness as being an element of grieving but now, it was taking down walls and creating new openings.

"Losses are hard, Grieving is hard. This unusual COVID period asked me to stop. It gave me time. I found forgiveness and freedom for myself."

Grief and Resilience

Both Mary Shelley and Susan Tilsch hint at resilience without using the word. Shelley says her protagonist experiencing nature gave him a sense of purpose in *The Last Man*. Tilsch speaks about freedom, the freedom to live while continuing to grieve her profound losses.

Minx Boren too expresses her understanding that human resilience and growth are the results of experiencing and expressing unending ambiguous grief in her untitled poem.

"we must learn

to hold it all

the flowers and the weeds

the raging fires and the seeds

we must find ways

to attend to it all

all that is dying or being destroyed

and all that is struggling to arise

from the ashes of despair

we must deeply feel each loss

and deeply embrace all that is

wanting to emerge

and God willing surge

we must learn

to love it all

or be depleted beyond

redemption by the virulence

of despair"

____

____

____

____

____

Here is Katrina Freese looking back at her experience and learning from COVID-19 when she was just seventeen.

> "My experience of COVID as a young woman about to graduate from high school was similar to that of many of my peers. I was excited about an extended spring break and looking forward to enjoying the beautiful transition from winter into spring. As time

passed, I graduated high school from home, and spring turned into summer; life moved on. My original plan to go away for college changed; instead, I stayed home, completed college courses from my bedroom, and continued to work.

"At the start of COVID, I was working as a Life Enrichment Assistant in a nursing home just a block from my childhood home. During my senior year of high school, I had been taking college courses on campus at the local community college. My weekly schedule typically consisted of classes at the college in the morning and working at the nursing home in the afternoon or evening.

"I worked mainly on the Memory Care floor, a single long hallway filled with seniors, dimly lit but alive with residents seeking companionship. The day before the COVID lockdown began, I remember heading to work, completing my daily tasks, and, most importantly, spending time with the residents. While going about my activities, I overheard a nurse mention that one of our residents was showing signs of COVID.

"One particular resident, who often tried to follow us off the floor at the end of the day, stopped me as I grabbed my purse and headed for the door, and asked, 'Where are you going? When will I see you again?' I smiled and told her, 'I'll see you tomorrow.' I will always remember the confused and worried expression on her face as I turned to walk away.

"That evening my boss called to say that all activities were suspended because two more residents were showing COVID symptoms. She told me I could stay home for the next week while they figured out where staff support was needed, since group activities were no longer allowed.

"I don't remember exactly how long I stayed home before I was called back to work, but I do remember regularly checking my emails for updates: which entrance to use, how to properly wear PPE, and, most painfully, notifications about residents passing away. By the time I returned, more than half of the residents on the Memory Care floor had died from COVID, including the resident I had walked away from. I was never able to visit her before she passed. I never imagined I would lose so many of the residents I had grown up with.

"When I returned, the nursing home decided that the best role for Life Enrichment staff was to supervise in-person family visits. That's right! the nursing home allowed people to visit their dying loved ones, under the supervision of me, a high schooler at the time. I was expected to remind families that they were not allowed to come closer than six feet of their loved one. They couldn't kiss, hug, or even hold their hands as they said goodbye.

"I can't imagine now a 17-year-old telling people twice or three times her age that they couldn't properly say goodbye to their loved one; it did not go well. I would often pretend I didn't see them inching closer or kissing their loved one goodbye as their timed visit ended.

"Only a few residents survived the first, second, and third waves of COVID that tore through the small nursing home. I had started working there two years earlier, and although I knew not all the residents remembered me, they all had a huge impact on my life. It felt like I had lost all of my extra grandparents.

"I remember my parents worrying about me seeing people actively dying every day. I went to work - something I didn't fully understand at the time, as I do now. Looking back on my experiences in the nursing home, I've come to realize how profoundly affecting and, at times traumatizing, it was to witness so many people transition into new stages of aging or pass away.

"Even with the grief and loss, working with seniors continues to inspire me to be a better human being every day. I hope that when I am near the end of my own life, I will be able to look back and be proud of how I spent my time on this earth."

Maureen Mitchell, who belongs to the order of The Sisters of Mercy, writes about the cost of state regulations during COVID-19, that changed the sisters' ability to practice their traditional grieving rituals.

"The Institute of the Sisters of Mercy of the Americas experienced many losses to the COVID-19 epidemic. In the Northeast area alone, we lost several sisters. At 3:00 each afternoon I called all the sisters in the Northeast Community to tell them who of the sisters had contracted the deadly virus and their condition. On many of those calls I had to tell them that a certain sister or sisters had died.

"Like all groups of people, we had to observe state requirements regarding visiting and burial. Sisters were not permitted to visit even if they were in the same care facility. We could not observe our normal ritual practices honoring a sister's passing.

"Part of our traditional ritual practice is always to have someone be with a dying sister, and a group of sisters would gather to pray and sing songs of comfort. If a sister was in a care facility, the sisters in that facility would be in and out of her room sitting with her. During the pandemic a sister in a facility was alone. Perhaps a nurse on staff would be with her; however, we never knew for sure.

"When a death occurred, the sisters could not attend the funeral. State requirements dictated that only five people could be present, and the services had to be outside.

"Normally all able sisters would attend the wake and funeral liturgy for a sister. At the wake service we would do a prayer ritual, and sisters were invited to share their memories about the sister. Often the sister herself planned the liturgy listing in advance: the songs and readings she would like, and who she wanted to participate in the different parts of the liturgy. In just one year we buried over 20 sisters without any of our normal rituals.

"Our resilience and creativity helped us express our sadness and grief. We began having regular zoom gatherings following deaths where we sang, prayed and shared our memories. Although this was not our customary way, it helped us grieve our losses."

"Mastering the art of resilience does much more
than restore you to who you once thought you were.
Rather, you emerge from the experience transformed into a truer
expression of who you were really meant to be."

– Carol Orsborn, *The Art of Resilience,* 2010

Resilience and leadership were necessary components to sustain a large portion of our population during the pandemic. Healthcare workers at all levels found themselves in difficult, even life-threatening positions, for which they were totally unprepared. A nurse friend of mine worked in her hospital from the beginning of COVID-19. She reflects here about her personal struggles, her views about her hospital situation, and the difficulties faced by the nurses on her team.

> "The pandemic moved into the US rapidly leaving the health care system scrambling and unprepared to ready our services and staff for unfamiliar challenges. Health care professionals were confronted with direct care for Covid-19 patients. Those who worked in emergency rooms and intensive care experienced a unique requirement: to face their fears of transmission and the potential impact not only on themselves but on their families and loved ones. Countless others: social workers, care managers, counselors, provided care remotely to patients and families.
>
> "In order for these professionals to show up every day and perform their roles competently and with compassion, leaders on every level needed to stand shoulder to shoulder with their team members, providing guidance and support in new ways.
>
> "I quickly observed the emotional responses of fear, uncertainty and even panic among the staff. Some were apprehensive that they might carry the infection into their homes and cause serious or fatal conditions to their elderly and young family members.

They were caught in a bind when family members insisted that they stay in a hotel or move into the garage and remain isolated from the family.

"As a team leader, I was called upon to recognize and address the complex dynamics that arose in those circumstances, simultaneously ensuring that the quality of care provided to patients and families was never compromised.

"It was essential to ensure that my team felt absolute support in order for them to respond with creativity and efficiency. It was disconcerting to all of us that regulations seemed to change daily, sometimes within hours. Each situation required careful analysis in order to ensure compliance with regulations and ethical principles. This fostered a new depth of interdependence between staff and leaders.

"I sat with many staff members facing difficult conversations with patients' family members, helping them to problem solve, deciding about whether to bring their family member home for convalescence. There was so much uncertainty about prolonged periods of contagion and serious limitations in home care services.

"In some situations, staff were in communication with surviving family members regarding funeral arrangements when they had been unable to say goodbye to their loved one face to face due to the highly restrictive visitation policies. Funeral homes were inundated and delays were unavoidable, thus further complicating the grieving process.

"Fortunately, I could rely on the strength of my relationships with my team members and other leaders. As I listened carefully to individual worries, I felt a solidarity with each member of my team that I had never felt before. I reflected on the need for a leader to be a source of strength and security for the staff. I felt moved to cultivate deeper compassion and empathy for the turmoil that the staff members experienced as they strove to maintain professional excellence in these uncharted waters.

"To say that the experience was unique would be a serious understatement. It occurred to me that, unlike situations faced previously, team leaders and staff were facing identical problems in our professional and personal lives. And yet, we all needed to summon the resilience to meet our respective responsibilities every day.

"The words of Nelson Mandela served me as a guiding principle:

'It is always impossible until it's done.'"

____

____

____

____

____

Author of *Master of Change: How to Excel When Everything Is Changing, Including You; Embracing Life's Instability with Rugged Flexibility—a Practical Model for Resilience,* Brad Stulberg, coach, and writer for The *New York Times,* wrote to answer questions he had about people's response to change during Covid.

"It was February 2021. We'd all been living with Covid-19 for nearly a year. I was in my kitchen in Western North Carolina, doing my usual skimming of the day's news. Regardless of the publication, left, right or center, I kept coming across headlines written in the spirit of "When are we going to get back to normal?" They rubbed me the wrong way, though at the time I didn't know why.

"What followed for me was a deep dive into change: When we are faced with change, why is it that we try to get back to where we were? Should we? What does it mean to be solid and strong when everything is always evolving, including us?

"The answers led me to a radical rethinking of change and some new ideas on how to work with it: We don't need to surrender all agency in the midst of a shift, nor do we need to latch onto control, which is often a futile endeavor. Rather, we can be both rugged and flexible in the face of life's inevitable flux.

"Change is hard for many people, including me. And yet it is also unavoidable.... We were living in a time of intensifying and accelerating change, whether in the form of a pandemic, new technologies like artificial intelligence or a destabilizing climate. If we are to maintain our health, let alone have any chance at flourishing, we need to transform our relationship with change by becoming more active participants, understanding that we can shape change as much as it can shape us."

"The way to stay stable through the process of change

is by changing, at least to some extent.

If you want to hold your footing, you've got to keep moving."

- Brad Stulberg

____

____

____

____

____

I didn't know I would write what follows; it just appeared. I felt as if I'd been taken over, by a being wiser than I. I was no longer in charge . . .

"The world grew quiet,
Yet within the silence, Resilience was born."

– Anonymous

The date of this writing was August 15, 2024. Perhaps I was influenced by August 13th (corresponding to Tisha B'Av, the 9th day of the Hebrew month of Av this year), the anniversary when Jews worldwide fast and grieve the fall of King Solomon's Holy Temple in 587 BCE, the Second Temple in 70 CE, and all other tragic events in our history. It is a time of reflection on those historic losses.

… my words tumbled onto the page, as if my mind was a servant of some deep profound place in me that knew intuitively but not consciously - about generations of ongoing Jewish grief and resilience. Here's what I wrote:

> "As a cultural example of grief and resilience that I am personally a part of, I cite Israel, whose national strength is beyond amazing when surrounded by enemies in 2023, and for as many centuries back as our history goes. We've faced slavery and redemption, became the world's scapegoat, blamed for Jesus' crucifixion, massacred during the Crusades, expelled from Spain, charged with spreading the Black Plague, butchered in pogroms throughout eastern Europe and Russia for centuries, accepted as citizens in Western Europe and then rejected, and in WWII 6 million of us burned to ashes in Hitler's Holocaust ovens.
>
> "On October 7, 2023, Hamas attacked Israel, committing brutal rapes, beheading and burning babies, murdering some 1200 civilians, injuring many more, and taking 250 as hostages - more than 20 of them still living in dark tunnels: emotionally, physically and sexually abused, underfed, and psychologically beaten for over 460 days.
>
> "And the world was horrified! But by October 8, 2023, Israel was at fault, the evil occupier, and once again the object of world hatred.
>
> "And yet, and yet … Israel and Jews throughout the diaspora grieve this massacre as our tradition teaches us to grieve all others. We continue to be an international people - to live with

hope and resolve that finally after more than 3500 years we will survive in our ancient home as a modern nation.

"What explains this resilience, this powerful urge to live, to prevail as a holy people, no matter how the world feels and treats us?

"I believe it is our willingness to grieve as a people, to study Torah and practice our traditions in a cohesive community, observing rituals that support us all over the planet no matter our diverse beliefs and traditions.

"Having all young men and women serve in the IDF (Israel Defense Forces) binds them to their families, to their battalions, to their nation.

"With humility and gratitude, we continue to receive as part of our generational (DNA?) inheritance: the gifts of moral strength, study, dedication, humor, the capacity to resist, resilience, and to never relinquish hope."

"I marvel at the resilience of the Jewish people.
Their best characteristic is their desire to remember.
No other people have such an obsession with memory."

– Elie Wiesel

On August 1, 2024, James Spiro wrote "How Startup Nation and the IDF Support Each Other" on Michael Oren's *Substack* column. *Startup Nation,* a 2009 book by Dan Senor and Saul Singer, is about Israel's innovation and tech economy.

> "What can explain the surprising success of *Startup Nation* and its connection to the IDF? "In my time as a reporter in the country, one word kept on coming up: 'Resilience'. Anytime we're threatened, we become more Israeli… we become stronger, more dedicated, and more 'resilient'."

____

____

____

____

____

On May 25, 2025, I listened to a podcast featuring the mental health chief of the IDF. Dr. Lucian Laur spoke about creating the National Resilience Center in Tel Aviv. As a nation of only nine million, military men and women have needed to return to battle several times over the last year and nine months. Soldiers and their commanders attend this Center to learn techniques to be and stay resilient faced with the horrors and brutality of war. The hope is to save a generation of young people, so they will not only survive but thrive as individuals, keeping the Israeli people and the IDF humane and strong.

The F [Friends of the] IDF have built the first ever IDF National Center for Mental Health and Resilience, a dedicated facility for soldiers in need of therapy and support. "Sometimes, healing begins in the most unexpected way, like on four paws. Eyal, a veteran once housebound by severe PTSD, found a lifeline in Jadah, a specially trained therapy dog. Before Jadah, Eyal couldn't step outside. Now, he plays with his children, reconnects with his wife, and has reclaimed pieces of the life he thought were lost forever."

Dr. Laur is now teaching resiliency skills and programs to mental health officers at the Walter Reed National Military Medical Center in Bethesda and also teaching in NATO countries.

And finally, Tolstoy has his say on the subject, quoted by Meir Soloveichik in his article "...How Torah Changed the World":

> "The Jew has brought down from heaven the everlasting fire and has illuminated with it the entire world .... He whom neither slaughter nor torture of thousands of years could destroy, he whom neither sword nor inquisition was able to wipe off the face of the earth, . . . he who has been for so long the guardian of prophecy, and who transmitted it to the rest of the world—such a nation cannot be destroyed. The Jew is as everlasting as is eternity itself."

____

____

____

____

____

Since I began reading Pauline Boss' most recent book in which she writes of no end to grief but the promise of living with resilience, I see **resilience** everywhere, and **as the most important gift we can pass forward with our Covid legacy writing.**

Permission to Grieve and Expressions of Grief

We live in a time and in a society obsessed with "personal happiness" often at the cost of silencing sadness. Grief, pain, and vulnerability are bypassed or dismissed. In this rush to push forward, we have become a frozen people, unable to grieve.

One reader of Ann Napolitano's 2023 novel *Hello, Beautiful* thanked her for "articulating grief in a way I needed to heal after losing my dad and uncle to Covid in 2020."

In *The Washington Post,* columnist Tara Parker-Pope quoted her colleague and friend, Lena H. Sun, who lost her 90-year-old mother to COVID-19 and experienced the challenge of saying goodbye and grieving.

> "After talking to experts and reading about loss to help me cope, I'm understanding that grief — the intense emotion that often manifests in physical pain and feels overwhelming in the moment — can hit again and again. It's with you forever. But grief is different from grieving — how we learn to navigate life without our loved one. Social isolation and the sheer quantity of deaths during the pandemic made this process even harder."

____

____

____

____

____

Reading *A Chorus of Stones* by Susan Griffin, I came across a reference to the 'secret' about the battle of Dresden in 1945. I'd never heard of the battle or the city, although I minored in world history in college. Curious, I followed the thread forty years after World War II, to *Slaughterhouse-Five,* a novel by

Kurt Vonnegut, based on his experience as an Allied prisoner in Dresden. Once called 'Florence on the Elbe' because of its beauty and history, Dresden was designated a "free port" and was a refuge for over 300,000 people.

In two days of bombing in February of 1945, Dresden's center was bombed to rubble by the RAF and the US 8th Air Force. It set off fire storms that killed as many as 35,000. The ruins remind me of war-torn towns in Ukraine and Gaza today Echoes of these horrible events, like the ripple effect of a stone on water, live on within us whether we've acknowledged or grieved them or not.

We inherit not only personal but cultural and historical grief. Whether or not we name them, they live within us. Legacy writing helps us turn those 'stones' over, make visible what's been buried, and grieve what must be grieved.

That includes not just losses from COVID-19 but nature's losses that we hear about and see daily in the media: earthquakes, hurricanes, floods, tornadoes, wildfires, melting glaciers, lost species, contaminated air and water. . . how can we turn our backs on humanity's and earth's losses?

____

____

____

____

____

His publisher wrote of Francis Weller's book, *The Wild Edge of Sorrow*:

> "Those who work with people in grief, who have experienced the loss of a loved one, who mourn the ongoing destruction of our planet, or who suffer the accumulated traumas of a lifetime will appreciate the discussion of obstacles to successful grief work such as privatized pain, lack of communal rituals, a pervasive feeling of fear, and a culturally restrictive range of emotion."

Additionally, Weller himself wrote:

> "The work of the mature person is to carry grief in one hand and gratitude in the other and be stretched large by them.... Grief keeps the heart fluid and soft, which helps make compassion possible."

Leo Tolstoy wrote:

> "Only people who are capable of loving strongly can also suffer great sorrow, but this same necessity of loving serves to counteract their grief and heals them."

And Søren Kierkegaard reminds us:

"Our past shapes the person that we are today
for the good and the not so good. How we view
our past experiences both consciously and sub-consciously
shape how we approach life."

____

____

____

____

____

Carol Ferris, a healer and astrologer, shared her experience of early lockdown: breathing under a dogwood tree, finally able to feel sacred clarity in the air. Nature offered solace. But grief accompanied it: for the Earth, for our part in its suffering. She invoked Xi Wang Mu, the Queen Mother of the West in Chinese mythology, who weeps because her children will die. Her grief is cosmic and generative.

> "In early May 2020, the world was two months into a global shut down due to the emergence of a mysterious, lethal virus. People were falling ill and dying in China, in New York, in Italy, and to my north, in Seattle, Washington.
>
> "I remember younger friends and neighbors offering to pick up groceries for me: at 76, years old, I was in the demographic most likely to die. I remember I did not go out – at the beginning – at all.

"What did we know about the virus itself then? Did we even know it was spread airborne through breath, through sneeze and cough? We knew enough, as time went along, to know that the virus attacked the body's blood/lung interchange: death by drowning, by suffocation. I do remember my family's utter panic: we purchased small digital measuring instruments to constantly tell us our oxygen saturation levels and pulse rates (dead Covid giveaways). We knew enough to begin wearing masks. My neighbor Roberta got out her sewing machine and stitched up red and black plaid lumberjack masks for us. We hadn't yet learned about N95s. There were no effective medicines at that point, and no vaccines.

"The news – local, national and international – began to show daily death numbers, photos began to display dying moments in oxygen tents in emergency wards in hospitals around the world, staff encased in astronaut-like gear to protect them – 'essential workers' – from transmission. But nurses and doctors around the world were contracting COVID and dying of it too. People in my neighborhood stepped out on their front porches at 7 pm every night and blew horns and banged on pans in support of their courage and commitment.

"In the US, the CDC officials began to issue regular suggestions about limiting contact, masking up, washing hands, washing groceries. I remember, early on, a grocery delivery and washing a head of cauliflower wrapped in cellophane, jars of almond butter and bags of apples - after all, someone, or some 'Someone', had handled them, and what had been on those hands? There were stories about people who had fallen ill from pushing an elevator button loaded with virus. I bought boxes of rubber gloves and carried spares with me in the rare moments I ventured out.

"Because it was ok to walk in my neighborhood, I found myself on an exquisite Oregon summer day, under my neighbor's glorious, blooming creamy white dogwood tree. I looked up at its crown, completely brilliant under a true-blue sky, and I could SEE-dimension. I could SEE the larger ether the tree and I shared. There were no cars. There were no planes or contrails. There was only. . . air. We were breathing together, the dogwood and me.

"I was struck dumb. I thought: how long has it been since I was in clean, spacious, delicious, luminous, life sustaining AIR? And in a flash of memory, I remembered being 10 years old at the lake in northern Idaho, the hills of the white pine forest lit by summer Sun and reflected lake light – so luminous you could almost see every individual needle of an entire forest hillside. There was a deep silence except for the whicker of a jay or the rustle of a foraging chipmunk, because there were no competing noises - no roar of a power boat nor hiss of the kerosene lamps, because – no electricity. Everything was alive and breathing together.

"It was that moment in the dogwood's place and mine in the radiant clean moment that I wept for a life lost – not just my personal life – but a road not taken, life of every being on the planet, every frog, every leaf and petal and blade, every set of lungs, every beating heart – of a life of mutuality and reciprocity, where everything consumed could translate into something consumable by something else. A life of beauty, of rich clear brilliance – of simple air, earth, fire, water – unpolluted by speed, desire, ownership, manipulation – an inter-relational field of life, not death.

"When I got home from that walk, I read in our local paper about the latest measurements of air and water pollution. Absent a daily demand on our resources of cars on freeways, planes overhead, cloud storage of a billion photo albums, viruses, our most primary giver of life – air – was returning to levels of non-pollution unseen since measurements had been initiated.

"Grief: how had we, how could we, have done this to ourselves, to each other, to our children, our dogs, our orchards, our oceans? How – HOW – could it ever be undone, wound back? Could it?

"Would it really ask our death in order for the simpler basic structures of earth life to successfully reassert themselves? Could all the foot dragging of governments and corporations - could all the resistance from the rest of us still unable to reduce our demands on our resources - could it give way to something simpler, life sustaining, eternal?

"And finally, I remembered the Xi Wang Mu, the Queen Mother of the West of ancient China, who symbolizes the carrying power of the feminine. While she is a human woman, robed and crowned by jade, she also has the ears and fangs and tail of a jaguar. She stands on a ledge before a cave on the sacred central Chinese mountain, Mt. Kunlun. And she is wailing. She is wailing so loudly she can be heard all over ancient China. She is wailing because she is going to bear children who will die. And now, we, like her, must trust that our death, and our grief, might lead to new life for our children and our children's children."

Patsy Glista, who lost her husband during Covid, graciously sent me four tender poems: "Precious," "Untitled," "Advice," and "Sobbing." They hold sorrow and light.

Precious

"Precious is the time we have

Precious are the moments we share

Precious are the faces

of grandchildren on the computer screen

or in front of me for real

Precious is the new flower bud

pushing its face to the sun

Precious are the moments

burned into our memory

Precious is the touch of the one I love

Remember– be kind, be patient, compassionate, tender

Precious moments are gone – all too soon."

Untitled

"In the beginning

I could not imagine

who I would be with you.

Now when you have

crossed that bridge

from dust to dust

I cannot imagine

if I can be without you

Would that I could, and yet –

You became a part of me

and I of you

Now for eternity enmeshed within my being."

Advice

"Voices, well meaning

Try this

Won't you come with us? Do

something new

Dust off a hobby

Join this group

Do things with friends.

When all I want to do

Is talk about you

To remember and retell

the stories of your life,

of our life.

Cementing them in my mind

before they fade

Lest they forget, lest I forget

All those precious moments

– Your words, your touch

The life you shared

That it was real

That it meant something

That you not be forgotten"

The following poem that Patsy Glista shared reminds me of Mary Shelley's protagonist in her novel, *The Last Man*, when in his grief, he experiences the resilience of nature and senses a purpose for living. Patsy concludes "Sobbing" with a tiny step of resilience, a glimmer of life and hope.

Sobbing

"I collapse to my knees at your grave

Tears pour out

my sorrows and sadness

Arms clutching granite

seeking solid ground

In time I clear away dead grass, and
trace my fingers over and over your name
My heart so heavy – literal pain
I give thanks for you
To the God we love

Turning, I breathe deep
a monarch butterfly flutters by
gently touring the cemetery
A pair of downy woodpeckers flit in the trees
Signs of life and hope"

____

____

____

____

____

Kathi Gowsell, a legacy facilitator from Canada, reflected in prose on the uncertainty, kindness, and wonder of 2020. Her refrain "I wonder..." echoes the constant beat of the pandemic. She writes:

All I Do is Wonder

"These days, it seems as though all I do is wonder. Yesterday I wondered about today. Today I wonder about tomorrow. I wonder what the future will bring. What will life look like post-COVID? Will there be a post-COVID or must we accept COVID as our new normal?

"I woke up this morning wondering about the rules. What's changed about what I can and cannot do today? Will masks become mandatory now? May I go out to dinner? Visit a library? I am confused by the decision of our provincial government to relax the rules around visiting our senior residences just as our positive tests are back on the rise. This is part of their "learn to live with COVID" plan and I have to ask, "What was the previous lockdown for?"

"I've never known a Canada so divided. Each province is judged by their COVID numbers. One province vilifies another. I read in the news this morning that hate incidents targeting Vancouver's Asians are up. I wonder how much more divided we will become.

"Women are behind men in recovering jobs lost during the shutdown of businesses. Childcare is less readily available at this time. Mom-guilt about trying to do it all is taxing the energy and stress levels of career women who are uncertain if and when they can return to the workforce. I wonder if COVID might exacerbate the inequality of the sexes.

"I wonder if I can stay optimistic about my children's future. Our national debt is over 1 trillion dollars. I looked it up. That's a 1 with 12 zeros! How will the government plan to service this debt? Will the kids ever experience the good times Paul and I did as young adults? Will they continue to have the freedom we've enjoyed?

"When will I see my sister again? I wonder when our border with the U.S will reopen to non-essential travel.

"Looking toward the future is like looking into a fog. I wonder what will emerge out of that fog. My hopes and dreams are suspended somewhere within it. When will making plans feel possible again

"Every day I wonder at so much.

"I wonder at:

- the arts: the poets who so eloquently put my COVID experience into words, the musicians who bring us joy through virtual concerts, the writers who lighten the mood and make me laugh or think a little more deeply,
- how writing and doodling in my journal feeds my soul,
- the innocence of young children and how they help adults focus on what truly matters, sunshine and nature and how the

earth takes care of herself when the movement of humans is restricted,

- at the ingenuity of entrepreneurs to pivot in what seems like a moment to keep their businesses alive and provide jobs.

"I especially wonder at the effect of human touch, the instant smile and warm feeling from the top of my head to the tips of my toes when I finally hugged my children.

"I am in awe of the kindness, patience, grace and goodness of people during what seems like an insurmountable situation.

"I think about where I'll fit in as time goes by. I can choose to wonder about possibilities. I can smile, I can listen, I can choose to be part of the solution by insisting that my beliefs hold true.

"Perhaps COVID has been sent to test my core beliefs. Love is all there is. The universe rewards action. Everything happens for a reason. Everyone needs a creative outlet. What you put out is what comes back.

"I wonder, if I focus on my beliefs today, will it make a difference tomorrow?

____

____

____

____

____

As we move through grief and silence, we reach toward something larger: an invitation to live differently.

"The deeper our wounds, the more likely they are to break us open into a greater sense of wholeness and compassion. Suffering, if we can find its meaning, often becomes the seedbed for new life."

— Parker J. Palmer

Chapter 5 gathers expressions of that new life. These are not stories of recovery in the traditional sense. They are not about "getting over" loss. Rather, they reflect how people, individuals and communities, have chosen to live more deeply into meaning.

Francis Weller wrote that ritual, imagination, and community are essential to processing grief. The following writers offer glimpses of what that looks like: how resilience can emerge through creativity, relationship, humor, and slowing down.

Whether planting a garden, holding a yoga pose on Zoom, or whispering gratitude into a pot of clay, each expression becomes a kind of offering. These stories remind us that even amidst global sorrow, we are still creators, still lovers, still capable of living a life of meaning, still capable of grace.

As you read what follows, I invite you to notice what echoes in your own experience. What have you done differently since the world changed? What have you noticed, honored, or created? What might you offer the future as part of your legacy?

Chapter 5: Beautiful Discoveries: The Gifts of Covid

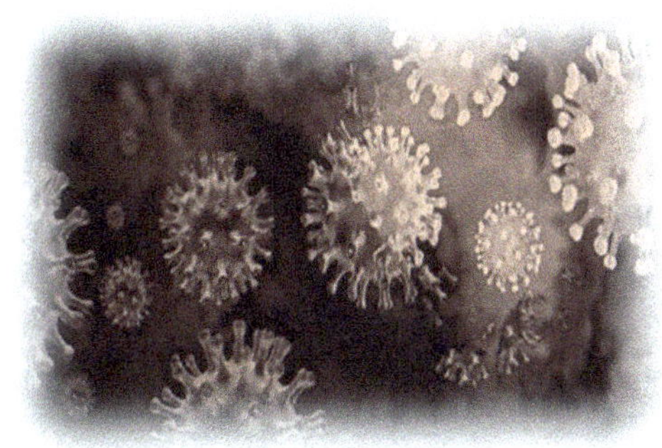

"An old woman planting an olive tree was asked
if she expected to benefit from its fruit or its shade.
She responded that she wasn't planting for herself,
but for her grandchildren.
"I found fully grown trees in the world.
As my ancestors blessed me,
so I bless the future
by planting for the generations to come."

– A Feminist Commentary derived from the Talmud
– Rachael Freed

"There are two ways of spreading light: to be the candle or the mirror that reflects it."

– Edith Wharton

We hear it all the time: "COVID fatigue." And it's true. Many of us grieved alone, were denied goodbyes, feared every cough, and saw young people miss social milestones, and have their education interrupted. We still carry the weight of what we couldn't control or comfort.

When I hear people say they 'can't wait til everything's back to normal', I cringe, knowing the past is gone and our future uncertain. Writer Susan DeFreitas reflected on the pandemic work of Ursula Le Guin:

"...if one thing is certain, it's this:

We cannot go back to the world we inhabited before the pandemic.

Not only because the threat the virus poses may never end,

but because time itself has changed us."

____

____

____

____

____

Arundhati Roy, Booker Prize author and activist, wrote an inspiring essay that appeared in *YES! Magazine*, expressing both what we began with in 2020 and the hope for a different future. Here is an excerpt of her powerful thoughts:

"What is this thing that has happened to us? It's a virus, yes. In and of itself it holds no moral brief. But it is definitely more than a virus....It has made the mighty kneel and brought the world to a halt like nothing else could. Our minds are still racing back and forth, longing for a return to 'normality', trying to stitch our future to our past and refusing to acknowledge the rupture. But the rupture exists. And in the midst of this terrible despair, it offers us a chance to rethink the doomsday machine we have built for ourselves. Nothing could be worse than a return to normality. Historically, pandemics have forced humans to break with the past and imagine their world anew. This one is no different. It is a portal, a gateway between one world and the next. We can choose to walk through it, dragging the carcasses of our prejudice and hatred, our avarice, our data banks and dead ideas, our dead rivers and smoky skies behind us. Or we can walk through lightly with little luggage, ready to imagine another world. And ready to fight for it."

The potential for new or renewed joys, the time to reflect about who we really are and what we value, is a start. All has not been destructive loss during the pandemic. Among those who've lost their jobs, their freedom, their way of life, their health, their loved people, there are others who had alternative experiences during COVID-19.

Some found space for stillness. Others for creativity. Some became reacquainted with their bodies, their gardens, their children. People painted, baked, planted, healed, rested. Many developed spiritual practices, deeper relationships, and unexpected wisdom.

In cities, empty buildings found new purpose. With empty offices and closed shops and restaurants 'new cities,' were created; office buildings converted to high-rise apartments, pedestrian ways were reenvisioned for what city centers can be for, its citizens. In homes, many found a slower rhythm. And within hearts, some felt clarity that had long been elusive.

Master legacy facilitator Judith Beier shared a letter she wrote to her adult daughters. Her pandemic reflection weaves love, listening, and the sacred turning inward. It closes with a blessing so personal yet universal. it could belong to every one of us.

> "Dear Kalia and Alyssa,
>
> "There was a time when I moved fast - quicker than my body wanted me to, quicker than I knew how to slow. I was teaching, parenting, striving, doing—all heart and fire, pouring everything I had into what I loved. And for a long while, it worked. Sort of.
>
> "But my body had been whispering to me for years. And I wasn't yet someone who knew how to listen. Not really.
>
> "It wasn't until menopause, until I felt the deep exhale of my life beginning to take shape in a new way, that the invitation to slow

became something I could no longer outrun. I couldn't hold everything anymore: two jobs, endless energy, the push. Something in me softened. Something in me asked to be heard.

"WE, the beloved social justice club, was one of the hardest things to let go of. It had my whole heart. But the fatigue told me the truth: I couldn't do it all anymore. I was aching. I was tired. And I was being asked to honor that.

"Then came the pandemic. The whole world slowed to a hush. And with it, so did I.

"At first, it was all urgency and scramble: those long days trying to convert a tactile, soulful teaching practice into pixels and links. But then, almost without warning, there was breath. Spaciousness. Longer lunches. Off-screen time. A loosening.

"There was nowhere to go, no way to perform productivity. And in that pause, something wild and holy began to root. I started to feel myself... really feel myself... for the first time in a long time. I began to dwell in my own body, not as a taskmaster, but as a beloved home.

"Meditation had taught me to sit still, but this... this was different. This was presence born of necessity and devotion. I moved slower. I heard the world more clearly. I came into rhythm with something ancient within me. And I liked it. I didn't want to go back.

"This listening: this sacred turning inward... became the altar I lived at. I began to ask my body what it needed and trust its answer. I honored my limits. I honored my light.

"In June 2023, I retired—earlier than made sense on paper, but in deep alignment with what I knew in my bones. Three days later, I got COVID. It knocked me down. I had no choice but to listen more deeply, more reverently. Everything was pared down to the essence: breath, presence, truth. What can I do? What is needed now? What is love asking of me?

"I kept surrendering. I kept listening. And over time, I noticed something had changed.

"I had changed.

"No longer chasing life, I found myself inhabiting it. Fully. Tenderly. With reverence. This sacred relationship with my own body, with the wisdom that lives there, has become one of the most profound teachings of my life.

"And now I offer it to you.

"My beloved girls, may you always know how to listen to your body as if it were a holy book. May you trust its guidance more than the noise of the world. May you slow down when you are called to, rest when you need to, and find that your light can burn steady... simmering, radiant, enough. May you honor the rhythm that is uniquely yours, even when the world moves differently. Especially then.

"I love you for always. Mama"

____

____

____

____

____

From her spiritual director, who died alone during the pandemic, Susie Kaufman received a spiritual gift. She describes here both her loss and her gift:

> "Recently, I attended some of the sangha zoom meetings, a group affiliated with the Plum Village tradition in Buddhism. Participants in this group, who are connected and rooted in the practices of Thich Nhat Hahn, are themselves representative of multiple traditions.
>
> "One person from the rotating cadre of facilitators always begins the sit with an invitation, welcoming all of us to recognize the rightness of our presence. This welcome goes on for quite some time since there are so many ways that we are The Same but Different. Every time I hear it, I feel a great weight lifting off my shoulders.
>
> "I feel bathed in Spirit. It always reminds me of Virginia, my spiritual director, who died of Covid, saying goodbye to her family on FaceTime from her quarantine inside a New Jersey nursing home. Virginia's outer world had shrunk to the dimensions of her bed, but I feel certain that her inner world was limitless.

"She taught me how to air out my spiritual linen and stretch my capacity to change and engage Otherness so I didn't live out my life in the stuffy, narrow confines of Sameness."

A. Stuart Hanson, who secluded with his wife in Wisconsin's North Woods, wrote of nature's indifference to the pandemic. He tapped maple trees, tended a vegetable garden, watched a doe teach her fawn to forage. His time in solitude became a season of gratitude.

"When a microscopic organism began to challenge every person on earth, my Gail and I were fortunate to be able to seclude ourselves in a cabin at the end of a gravel road on the edge of the Great North Woods of North America. The cabin was isolated but we had access to telephones, internet, and cable television which were not affected by the virus.

"As the virus spread and began to take lives, especially the elderly, we followed with fear, personal vulnerability, and the horror of the worldwide pandemic.

"On the other hand, we were submerged in nature. As the snow began to melt in late March of 2020 in Northwest Wisconsin, the sweet sap in maple trees began to flow. It begged to be collected and boiled down to a delicious syrup. The vegetable garden reappeared in April and asked to be revived and replanted. In May a doe brought her fawn to our yard to teach it to forage when it wanted to suckle. The nature of the woods didn't know there was a virus about.

"Gradually warmer weather filled the trees with leaves and our lake became warmed for swimming. We waved at passing boaters but had no visitors on land. By the time the nights began to cool in September, we knew more about this deadly virus. It wasn't spread by surfaces or anything we could see. It was spread by the air infected persons exhaled. Six feet of separation was not enough. Groups of people who shared their air also shared the virus.

"As the fall colors filled the woods, we began to feel more comfortable. A vaccine was on the horizon as the leaves began to fall. Freezing nights gave us the first snowfall. It was time to return to the city before we were snowed in.

"We reflected on our months in the woods. Nature had shown us its annual cycle up close. Our understanding of our place in the world was challenged and expanded. Both the virus and nature's transitions made us humble and grateful to be alive"

____

____

____

____

____

Michael Ziomko, a retired corporate executive and potter, spent silent hours in his studio, shaping bowls for community hunger events. For the first time, he found new meaning in his 'making' of pots, and he began to bless the clay. His words:

> "My retirement and the pandemic coincided. I knew I would be alone more anyway; the pandemic just confirmed it, beyond imagination.
>
> "It focused me. I'm a potter, and my detached garage is my studio. I knew I would be spending a lot of time in the studio but now the time is different. I have for the last year and a half been working in the studio in silence, which means no music. But somehow, in some way I can't characterize, the silence or the times have made me look at my work very differently.
>
> "I learned how to make pots almost 50 years ago, mostly functional pots: dinner ware, serving sets, platters, and covered jars. But my focus in the last several years has been making bowls for 'Empty Bowls' events.

"This is an event that features a meal of soup, that you enjoy eating from a handmade bowl in a communal setting. You donate to help feed people, and you leave with your bowl, now empty, as a reminder that you have helped to fill the empty bowls in your neighborhood. In short, it's an event that encourages community mindedness while raising money to feed people. I donated my bowls for many such events.

"The point is – I've made thousands of such bowls, and you would think there's nothing more for me to learn about making 'my bowl'. Each is generally the same shape and size. But this past winter, I began to do things in the making process I'd never done before, subtle things.

"For the first time, I started to watch the pot grow, in the making process, from the top. I came to think of it as the overview perspective, rather than from the side, which was how I had learned and what I had been doing for decades. This different way of looking at the formation of the pot changed everything....

"In addition, I inscribed sayings on the inside of my bowls, such as 'blessings on you'. This meant that I had to invent a calligraphic style. It is the part of finishing the bowl that means the most, incising the words into clay. For the first time, I decided to re-dampen the clay right before I incise the words into it. A simple thing, again, that I might have been doing all along, but never did. This has increased the meaning and the pleasure of the making, beyond words....

"Further, the dampening process has required that I touch the pot again, delicately, tenderly, quietly, and slowly. It is a way for me to bless the pot, like I never have before....

"I guess what I'm saying is that somehow, the pandemic helped
me to see things differently,
to do things differently,
to feel things differently,
and most importantly, to be open to all of these new differences."

____

____

____

____

____

Viktor Frankl, survivor of three concentration camps and author of *Man's Search for Meaning*, believed that our primary motivation as humans is to find meaning in life. Remarkably, he wrote, having spent more than three years in the camps, where his parents, brother and wife were murdered:

"I never would have made it if I could not have laughed.
It lifted me momentarily out of the horrible situation,
just enough to make it livable."

Laughter, in the face of grief, is a kind of resilience. Perhaps we can understand Frankl's ability to laugh when we read the Mayo Clinic's suggestion that laughter can make it easier to cope with difficulties. Research shows that laughter can provide a good internal physical workout, defuse tension, lower blood pressure, even improve immunity. A sense of humor and the ability to laugh provides us with a break from the spell of loss and can be healing. Dostoyevsky wrote:

"If you wish to glimpse inside a human soul and get to know the man, don't bother analyzing his ways of being silent, of talking, of weeping, or seeing how much he is moved by noble ideas; you'll get better results if you just watch him laugh. If he laughs well, he's a good man.... All I claim to know is that laughter is the most reliable gauge of human nature."

– Feodor Dostoyevsky

Carol Weinstock shared humorous poems that she wrote early in the pandemic; playful reminders of our strength in silliness and our power in play. "We are all superheroes," she wrote. "We wear masks not to fight crime, but COVID-19."

Masks

"Hi ho, Silver, away!

and the Lone Ranger

rides off, black mask circling his eyes.

Spiderman shoots web magic

as he hides behind

his full-face mask.

Batman rules Gotham City,

face covered in a

stern, impassive mask.

Paper or cloth, we wear masks

to fight not crime

but Covid 19.

We are all superheroes!"

Hey, Covid!

"Hey. Covid!

Yeah. I'm talkin' to you.

You with the purple spikes.

You think you can sashay in here

and take over the world,

sauntering around like

a brazen hussy.

You think just because
you've recruited variant
punks from Brazil, India
and Britain that you're
the conquering hero.

Well, I have news for you!

Our doctors, nurses,
researchers, caregivers
are armed and ready to
take you down. Armed with
vaccines and science.

Your spikes will split
before our needles.
It takes only a poke,
a jab, a shot into
willing, waiting arms.

Soon, very soon,

you'll join your

low life brothers

the bubonic plague,

the Spanish flu, polio

in the dustbin of

medical history.

So long, sucker!!"

"Earth laughs in flowers."

-Ralph Waldo Emerson

James Parker, wrote in *The Atlantic* on April 19, 2020, giving us his lyrical "Corona Prayer," a reminder of humor, humility, and awe during a time of uncertainty:

"Dear Lord,

In this our hour of doorknobs and droplets,
when masks have canceled our personalities;
in this our hour of prickling perimeters, sinister surfaces,
defeated bodies, and victorious abstractions,
when some of us are stepping into rooms humid with contagion,
and some of us are standing in the pasta aisle;
in this our hour of vacant parks and boarded-up hoops,
when we miss the sky-high roar of the city
and hear instead the tarp that flaps on the unfinished roof,
the squirrel giving his hinge-like cry, and the siren constantly passing,
to You we send up our prayer, as follows:

Let not heebie-jeebies become our religion,
our new ideology, with its own jargon.
Fortify us, Lord. Show us how.
What would your saints be doing now?
Saint Francis, he was a fan of the human.

He'd be rolling naked on Boston Common.
He'd be sharing a bottle. No mask, no gloves,
shielded only by burning love.

But I don't think we're in the mood
for feats of antic beatitude.

In New York City, and in Madrid,
the saints maintain the rumbling grid.
Bless the mailman, and equally bless
the bus driver, vector of steadfastness.

Protect the bravest, the best we've got.
Protect the rest of us, why not.
And if the virus that took John Prine
comes, as it may, for me and mine,
although we've mostly stayed indoors,
well—then, as ever, we're all Yours.

Until further notice,

AMEN"

Peggy Thompson rediscovered a cherished friendship during lockdown; teaching art via Zoom, receiving Pilates in return, and deepening love across continents. "Best of all," she writes, "our friendship has flourished!"

"When I was twenty-one, I attended The School of the Art Institute of Chicago where I took an elective course, beginning modern dance. A fellow student, Sharon S, loved to dance and had a big warm smile. We became friends.

"As time passed, Sharon's father, a brilliant rabbi, decided to move his entire family to Israel. In Israel she changed her name to Sharone. We kept in touch, over the phone, about once a year.

"Then came COVID. As usual we called; now we were both in isolation. We were bored and lonely and we both needed hope and creativity to keep ourselves positive.

"We decided to trade our vocations. I would teach Sharone art and she would teach me Pilates! We zoomed each other every other week. For the first half hour we would talk about our lives like in the good old days. The trust was profound between us. The relationship deepened and the humor and warmth strengthened as we shared our journeys of aging, the worries about our grown children, the joy of a new grandchild.

"She showed me her beautiful art as she gained confidence, tried new materials and transferred her dance wisdom into visual composition and harmony of movement.

"And I learned Pilates!! Gentle but thorough, my body is strengthened because of it!

"And best of all, our friendship has flourished! I am so blessed because of COVID and the blessing of Zoom!"

____

____

____

____

____

Linda N. Spencer, in "The Colors of Stillness," journaled through her pandemic year in Barcelona. Silence reawakened her creativity. Writing became her way back to color, purpose, and self.

> "The Coronavirus, first appearing in Wuhan, China had migrated through humans to Europe and other countries worldwide. On March 14, 2020, Spain put a lockdown into effect, essentially closing its economy.
>
> "The Spanish government ordered people to stay indoors, except for going for groceries, to the pharmacy, to get medical care, or to walk a dog close to home. Businesses in Spain closed their doors, and suddenly the bustle and noise of a vibrant city fell silent. At the time, my husband and I were in Barcelona.
>
> "In those early days in Spain, we were horrified by the news reports of the deaths and illnesses in Madrid as the virus spread. We saw the monstrous wave that had started in China coming at us.
>
> "I learned that my emotions and thoughts are fluid, sometimes gentle, and other times intense. At that time, it was vital to focus on remaining centered in the face of something that was

confusing, and at times, frightening. This period was referred to by many politicians as a time of war, and the war was with an enemy we could not see but that was causing havoc in multiple ways.

"Many of us chose to take the lockdown as a time of reflection. That was the choice I made. I remember the first time I heard the birds chirping in Barcelona after the lockdown started. At first, the silence was deafening. It was strange, and the feeling was that it was almost post-apocalyptic. Something enormous had occurred, and the silence was what remained.

"In that silence and that stillness, I searched… for my creative voice. I re-discovered that creativity and the arts, including writing, would become a grounding force for me. Writing was where I picked up the colors for my life when there was so much confusion and anxiety everywhere.

"I later realized that the stillness was producing more color-filled creativity in others. Painters painted. Musicians sang and wrote music. Writers wrote. Dancers danced… Creativity was everywhere I chose to look. All I had to do was turn on my computer or look at my social media feeds. Creative sharing was happening across space and time.

"I took online art history classes, watched world-class performances from musicians and saw French ballet dancers practice together both live streamed from their homes. There was sharing and a global sense of community despite the separation and stillness. The magic, if you chose to see it, came through technology, which served as a substitute for being live and in-person, and it inspired and offered so many of us bright colors in the stillness of our lives and darkness happening outside of our doors.

"While stillness is most certainly the word I would choose for this year, something else occurred after the lockdown in the summer of 2020. I thought that life would return to some form of normality as we'd known it. However, that was not the case.

"People spoke of a 'new normal' as mandated mask-wearing became a 'thing'. Sporting a mask in the hot summer is not something that anyone enjoys, and it curtailed my going out because of the oppressiveness during the heat of Spain. And so, more stillness.

"During what's been called the Great Pause, there's been a lot of stillness, which creates opportunities for reflection. The quiet the virus brought gave me a lot of room for thought. And one of the things that became apparent in my life is that it brought light and exposed shadows from the past that had always lurked, but I was too busy to face.

"One day, I realized there is so much to stillness in life… if I just listen. Being home for weeks also made me realize I had the time, without any excuses, to create for myself. And, for me, writing was that colorful creation. Like any other writer, I have an inner drive to create and express myself through words."

As the world paused, she writes, she heard birdsong, rediscovered Van Gogh and Josephine Baker, and realized she had always had time—but never the stillness.

> "We can hear things we may not have heard before we were still. For instance, my stillness ranged from hearing birds chirping to diving into the stories of artists and paintings. All this became color for me inside the apartment I shared with my husband and little dog, Bijou.
>
> "The silence of my life gave me space and time to consider ideas of interest to me from somewhere in the corners of my mind. There was never enough time to contemplate them–until there was–during the lockdown.
>
> "Nah, the reality is that I did have the time to contemplate before the pandemic, but the lack of stillness made many other things in my life a higher priority. Thinking of Van Gogh or Josephine Baker when things were normal before this pandemic seemed wasteful of time. There was always a life to be lived. The color of my life, and perhaps that for many people, was outwardly focused and involved things we did outside of ourselves. The situation we found ourselves in early 2020 allowed many of us to look at the colors inside of ourselves.
>
> "The lockdown and 2020 turned out to be one of the most significant periods of my life, as it has been for many people. It was only because of the oddity of that year and my realization that the space created for creative solidarity could be mine."

And now we arrive where this book has always been leading: to you, the reader. I have been so inspired by those whose reflections have personalized all the themes of this book. In prose and poetry, they've shared their fears, loneliness, grief, resilience, and the positive learning and gifts of COVID-19. I hope that their courage and openness will encourage you, whether you've ever considered writing to your family and future generations before, to write your own reflections about this still unfinished pandemic and its ramifications.

Susanna Schuerman, a master legacy facilitator, offers this final poem: may it inspire you to write your legacy letters. To name your truth. To bless the future.

"THIS IS OUR TIME

to weave the threads that hold generations together

to shine the light of the soul

THIS IS OUR TIME

to open our hearts

to restore balance

to strum the chords of harmony

THIS IS OUR TIME

to listen to the wind that carries the whispers and warnings of the past

while singing the future into being

with every word you write.

Because you hold the memory of the past

and the dream of our future

you are the one(s) who have the tools to build the bridge

between the past and future.

Our job is to bless and be blessed.

To reap and to sow at the same time.

Our job is to nurture the spiritual flame that burns in all of us
with stories of courage, hope, beauty, and delight.
Our job is belonging.
We help create sanctuaries and circles
where stories of the heart can be listened to and reflected upon.
Our job is to make a difference
as we encourage and offer people a way to home, to themselves.
Our job is to create remembrances
as we harvest stories from the seasons of our lives.
Our job is to create space to be known and to be heard,
that our values are shared and clarified.
Our job is to create opportunities to celebrate life."

"Coronaflower"

By

Artist, Adam A. Werth

Rachael's Blessing to the readers of *Life and Loss*

My hope for each of you readers and writers is contained in my blessing:

May you continue to honor the links between the past and the future through this sacred, ancient tradition of legacy writing.

May each and all of you be blessed with the lessons and wisdom COVID-19 bequeathed us, healed by your courage to grieve what you lost, and the resilience to move forward in your lives with humor, gratitude, compassion, and love; for yourselves, others you love, and our magnificent planet.

Appendix I: A Brief Pandemic History: Context for COVID-19

We're hurt more deeply when we don't know—and when we don't remember. To place COVID-19 in context, we need to understand the long history of pandemics, the facts and feelings they carried, and the lessons each left behind. If we fail to preserve our past, how can we fulfill our responsibility to future generations? This appendix provides us with some knowledge about earlier pandemics and the ease with which we 'forgot'.

That's right: COVID-19 is not the first ... or only ... pandemic in human history!

What do you know about the Spanish flu a century ago, a pandemic that occurred during a time of deep societal silence?

Laura Spinner, in her book *Pale Rider*, called the 1918 flu epidemic "the true lost generation" suggesting the little-known catastrophe forever changed humanity.

Robin Cook in *Pandemic* chastised his readers: "Haven't you ever heard of the 1918 flu pandemic? It killed more people than World War One and World War Two combined."

In my research I found almost nothing written about the emotional and mental aftermath of the Spanish flu: no record of mass grief or family trauma, no intergenerational mental-emotional suffering documented about the millions of families affected by this highly contagious virus. Little public health or governmental support was provided during or after the pandemic subsided. Most of the resources and attention focused on wounded soldiers returning from WWI.

Surprisingly, a New South Wales newspaper reported that in the United States all places of public entertainment were closed, even bars and public telephones. Church services were cancelled, and mask-wearing in public was mandatory, apparently without political controversy, but it is not known how many people's lives were saved because of these measures.

Earlier pandemics were even more catastrophic. The Black Death—the bubonic plague—decimated Europe and the Mediterranean. In 1349, Frederick the Great blamed and burned Dresden's Jewish population, believing they brought the plague. Between 1346 and 1353, the global population plummeted from 475 million to as few as 350 million.

Smallpox, discovered in mummies as early as 1156 BCE in the Ramses V era, has been rampant ever since. Over 400,000 people died yearly in the 18th century in Europe. Dr. Edward Jenner's vaccine developed in the 1790s led to its global elimination in 1978, according to WHO and the CDC.

There were others throughout history, and even in the 20th century. Polio crippled children across the U.S. during the 1940s and 1950s. Each year, it killed 6,600 and paralyzed 119,000. There was no cure.

> My memories of that time are limited: I remember the March of Dimes fundraising campaigns, when I raided my piggy bank to fill cards in our elementary school to help polio research. I later learned that FDR had been permanently crippled with polio. I recall seeing terrifying pictures of children in "iron lungs" –

images that likely influenced my decision to change my advance directive to refuse a ventilator if I contracted COVID-19.

I knew that paralysis was a common outcome of the virus. A friend of mine contracted polio when we were five. She was left permanently weakened in one arm and leg; perhaps many of her health issues as a woman almost 87 are long term effects of that early illness.

In the summer of 1946 when I was eight, I was sent to camp in Michigan for a month with three cousins from Illinois. When the month was over, polio was not! It was still raging in Minneapolis, so my parents kept me at camp for an additional month. It was a confusing time for me, feeling lonely for my family, not understanding why I couldn't come home.

____

____

____

____

____

Philip Roth, in his novel *Nemesis* described the 1944 polio epidemic:

"Finally, the cataclysm began –
the monstrous headache, the enfeebling exhaustion, the severe
nausea, the raging fever, the unbearable muscle ache,
followed in another forty-eight hours by the paralysis."

Sister Kenny, an Australian nurse, developed hydrotherapy and passive exercise techniques considered radical at the time. In 1942, she opened the Courage Kenny Institute in Minneapolis, where her treatments proved lifesaving and mitigated paralysis. Meanwhile Dr. Jonas Salk developed a vaccine that essentially eliminated polio, until 2024, when the danger of a polio epidemic was found in Gaza. Israel provided almost a million doses to Gaza to inoculate children.

Then came the AIDS epidemic. Though HIV-AIDS began in the early 1920s, its connection to homosexuality kept it in the shadows. Many people had no idea it existed. Yet by 2021, AIDS had taken over 40 million lives. The 1993 film, *Philadelphia,* starring Tom Hanks, brought AIDS pain and stigma into the mainstream. Hanks won an Oscar for his portrayal of a dying AIDS patient, and the world began to awaken. Still, homophobia remains a persistent prejudice in our country. Today, thanks to medical advancements, 39 million people worldwide live with HIV.

Enough about what we don't know about pandemics; let's get to the history of the ethical will (legacy letters) so we can, finally, begin writing our own legacy letters.

Appendix II: History of the Legacy Letter (Ethical Will)

The ethical will was created by rabbis as they studied the *Hebrew Bible*. In the final verses of *Genesis* as he lay dying, Jacob gathered his 12 sons, blessed them, imparted his wisdom, and asked them to take his remains to be buried in the land of Canaan where his ancestors were buried.

Centuries later rabbis used this story as a model to encourage men of their communities to write what they called an "ethical will" to bless their sons, transmit ethical instructions to future generations, and express their dying wishes.

When I began helping women to write their wisdom, blessings, and dying wishes (legacy letters) at the end of the 20th century, almost no one had heard of an ethical will. Unlike the two legal wills (the will of valuables and the "living will" or advanced directive), the ethical will is not a legal document. It is a personal document of values.

Women, in particular, often doubted they had anything important to share. For example, "I was just a mother who raised four kids," many said. I reminded them that all of us have written letters—and that's what we would be writing. I began calling these writings "legacy letters." I kept the three central elements from antiquity as the foundation for modern legacy letters:

1. Passing down the wisdom gained through lived experience
2. Offering blessings
3. Expressing end-of-life wishes (when appropriate)

Anna Quindlen, interviewed about her 2022 book, *Write for Your Life,* said:

> "Most of the history we know has been written by prosperous white men in positions of power about great events. But as a mother, grandmother and friend, I want intimate history. I want to know how people like me got up in the morning and lived their lives during .... COVID-19 years, during the civil war in India, in Ukraine .... That kind of history is only available to us if ordinary people write about their lives...People find it more accessible to do this in letter form because they're thinking of the reader as someone who they love and who loves them."

Our letters can address many topics: COVID-19 or other major events of our time, to provide generational family history, ask forgiveness, share a secret, put our lives in order, convey gratitude to those who helped us along our way, what we know about aging, and more.

"About blessings: I'd just begun working with legacy letters when I was invited to address a group of elders. They came by bus and I had just 55 minutes to clarify legacy writing with them. I decided to provide a quick overview and then talk about blessings. I gave each of them a 4 x 6 index card and a pencil. After I finished my presentation, I asked them each to write a blessing to someone who needed a blessing at this time. When they'd finished, I asked them, if they chose, to say who the blessing was for and to share their blessing.

"I'd noticed as they wrote – there were about a dozen sitting in a circle – that the two women to my direct left had not written a word. Thus, I started the sharing with the people on my right. Every one of them had something to share, and all were touched by the depth of the blessings they heard.

"Then we arrived at the two women who hadn't written. I asked the first if she'd like to share. She replied rather condescendingly, "I didn't write". Here, as a beginner leading this work, I made a huge mistake! I asked her simply, 'Why not?' and then she spoke up, expounding in a confident voice, that only priests, ministers, and rabbis can bless people.

"I was speechless. Then I glanced up and the clock showed five minutes to the hour. I pulled myself together, thanked them all for coming, and announced that their bus was waiting, and it was time for them to board.

"After they left, I thought: 'I didn't even have the wherewithal to suggest that we bless each other when we sneeze!'"

____

____

____

____

____

Here are some biblical moments when a (heavenly or earthly) 'father' blessed his people:

> Exodus 19: Revelation. . . God convenes the Israelites giving His blessing and instruction (the Torah) to his children, the Israelites, at Mt. Sinai.
>
> Exodus 39:42 When the Israelites completed building the Tabernacle in the wilderness, Moses blessed them.
>
> Matthew 5: Jesus blessed his disciples (Sermon on the Mount).

Our documents 'legacy letters' stay faithful to the content of old in order that our contemporary voices and values express our deepest and highest messages and blessings to the future.

Appendix III: Getting Down to the Business of Legacy Writing

As legacy writers one of our purposes is to learn from our experiences within our families, communities, and the wider world, and then to share our understanding so that future generations might benefit from our wisdom. Perhaps they'll be better equipped to handle the events and ambiguous grief of a future pandemic because of what we choose to write today.

A Writing Exercise: Looking at How You Coped

As you've read the diverse COVID-19 reflections, poems, legacy letters, and Elliot Kirschner's essay with their wide range of descriptions, perceptions, insights, humor, grief, resilience and spiritual growth, I expect you are eager to reflect and write about your own experiences.

Before writing a pandemic legacy letter, I suggest doing a preliminary writing exercise to unlock and recall your memories, thoughts and feelings, your grief, and the coping skills you used during COVID-19.

"Life can only be understood backwards,

But it must be lived forwards."

- Søren Kierkegaard

Write for no more than 30 minutes at a sitting. You can return to your writing later ... perhap s i n a da y or two ... to reread, reflect, and revise. It's likely you'll wa nt to add new thoughts or delete those that no longe r feel rele vant.

Below are a number of prompts. Some will speak directly to your heart; others may not apply. Let them guide you toward what's most personally meaningful.

Continue to explore ideas from this exercise and the notes you wrote in the body of this book responding to other people's writing until you feel ready to write a legacy letter.

You may write in short phrases or notes; this is not about perfect grammar or full sentences. It's about freeing your voice. You can edit later.

Find a quiet place to write where you won't be disturbed. Read through the list slowly and when an idea or memory is awakened, jot it down.

Prompts for Reflection

1. What did I do with "my time" for the last COVID-19 years? What could I and did I do for others?

2. What's been the hardest thing for me about living during the pandemic?

3. If I contracted COVID-19, what were my physical, emotional, mental and communal experiences? And what was my recovery like?

4. How did my relationships change during the pandemic? What and whom did I miss most–and why? How did I deal with my need to belong? Did Zoom, WhatsApp, social media and television have positive or negative effects on me?

5. Did I lose anyone close to me? Do I know someone who did? Was I aware of my grieving and how did I express it? What if anything provides me solace? What is my life like without them? Have I noticed any growth in my resilience?

6. What external changes affected me personally during this time?

7. What was my greatest fear during this time? Do I still feel the impact of those fears or other anxieties?

8. What was my greatest joy during this time?

9. What hopes and dreams do I have–for myself and for those I love–as we transition to an unknown future? Do I believe they will come to pass?

10. Write about your feelings during this time and how you dealt with them:

> (alienation, anger, anxiety, depression, fear, grief, guilt, hopelessness, lethargy, loneliness, loss of purpose, sadness).
>
> And my positive feelings:
>
> (gratitude, hope, humor, joy, resilience, appreciation of nature, of life, and renewed purpose or insight, increased spirituality).

11. How did non-human companions ... nature, gardens, pets, trees, art and music ... affect me? Have I developed new interests, pastimes or hobbies?

12. Where did my hope come from during the pandemic? From faith, nature, family, friends, observing others' resilience?

13. What changed in my life? What changes have I made in myself, to my surroundings, my work, with my friends, family, and other relationships in response to COVID-19?

14. What did I lose during the pandemic? What benefits, however unexpected, did it offer me? Consider growth through grief and the development of resilience.

15. Do I (or did I) believe in God? Has my spiritual life changed during COVID-19? If so, how?

Did my attitudes about mortality change during the pandemic? If so, how?

16. And finally, what is the most important message I want to share with my grandchildren or future generations about this time? Paint a word picture for readers 60–75 years from now.

May you and your writing be blessed.

Appendix IV: Tips and Tools for Legacy Letter Writing

Size and Shape

Each legacy letter is unique in both content and purpose. A legacy letter can be as short as one page and take less than 20 minutes to write. Set manageable goals. I recommend writing for no more than 20–30 minutes at a time. The emotional content can be deep. Let your words and your body rest between sessions. You may want to set it aside for a day or two, and return to it with fresh eyes to edit, add thoughts, or remove something you no longer feel belongs.

Other letters may grow into short books, taking months to complete…especially when researching family history or expanding on broader themes.

And of course, most letters fall somewhere in between. There is no right or wrong length.

Beyond Words

You may wish to include visual elements:

- Photographs
- Illustrations
- Family handwriting samples
- A cherished recipe
- A favorite song or hymn
- A eulogy

If your letter is intended for more than one person, you might keyboard the original (or type as we elders say) but be sure to **sign each copy in your own hand** and consider including a handwritten note at the end of each copy. Our handwriting is as unique as our fingerprints, and personalizes the invaluable gift you are offering.

About Tone

Avoid directing anger at a specific person, unless the anger is an essential part of your COVID experience and necessary to include. Anger, while a natural component of grief, may be more appropriately expressed in your private journal or therapeutic writing. Why?

Because fifty years from now, a descendent reading your legacy letter may not understand the context, nuance, or purpose of that emotion. Anger can also obscure the deeper wisdom and compassion you intend to share in your legacy.

Balancing Heart and Head

Write with your **heart**. Edit with your **head**.

Check whether your blessing is in fact a blessing (coming from your heart) or is it an instruction (coming from your mind)?

This is especially important when composing your final paragraph, the blessing. If your "blessing" sounds more like an instruction, return to your heart and let your genuine love and hope guide your words.

Additional Guidelines

- Always **date your writing**–and any future edits or revisions. This provides context and continuity.

- **Decide** who should receive your COVID-19 legacy letter(s), and when.

  Will you offer it to a loved one now, to open a conversation? (My advance directive addition given to my children–about not wanting a respirator opened a whole new avenue of conversation for us focused on how they would prepare for my dying.)

  Will you address it to a future generation, with instructions to open it after your death? If so, place it with other important papers and clearly label the envelope: "To be opened after my death by [Signed with your name]."

- **Set limits.** Given the emotional nature of this writing, I recommend writing for no more than 20–30 minutes at a time. Then stop. Rest. Let the writing sit overnight before returning to revise or continue.

- **Use only what serves you.** These suggestions are meant to support you. Follow only what resonates with your experience, values, spirit, purpose and voice.

- **This is your legacy letter. Trust it. Trust yourself.**

Appendix V: A Four Paragraph Template for Writing a Legacy Letter

You'll find this template described earlier in Chapter 1. It outlines the basic shape of one of my personal legacy letters. The structure includes four essential elements:

1. A context-setting paragraph
2. A story or reflection
3. A lesson, value or insight – your wisdom
4. A closing blessing

This simple structure helps guide your writing and provides coherence and meaning to your letter.

The Template:

No matter the content a template provides a structure, making writing legacy letters simpler and less daunting. A legacy letter using this framework can often be completed in four paragraphs in about 20-30 minutes. Feel free to use this as a guide and adapt it to your own voice and purpose:

Paragraph 1: Context

A wise mentor once told me, "All texts have a context." We are often unaware of the broader influences shaping our lives. Offering a framework for what follows gives your readers a snippet of family history, a snapshot of significant present and historical times, a meaningful frame for what follows, and provides depth to your personal reflection.

Paragraph 2: Story

All of us have unique stories ... deeply personal and shaped by our time and history. Sharing them helps us feel seen and known, creates belonging, connects us to past and future generations, and allows us to pass forward the insights and wisdom we've acquired. The story may recount a personal experience, an ancestral memory, a cherished tradition or ritual, an apology, an appreciation, or personal details about a major event like the COVID-19 pandemic. Use vivid details to make your story come alive. Your letter need not contain every story ... just one that matters right now.

Paragraph 3: Learning

This is where wisdom emerges. Reflect on the insight, value, or learning gained from your story. What personal truth will you pass forward? This is often the most meaningful part of the legacy letter, where your experience is transformed into a legacy ... a lasting gift for those who come after you.

Paragraph 4: Blessing

Offer a heartfelt blessing. This closing paragraph flows naturally from your story and reflection. It may include words of encouragement, protection, hope, or affirmation. As we bless others, we often find ourselves blessed as well.

The ancient ethical will originated from the biblical story of Jacob, who, before his death, blessed his twelve sons (Genesis 49). This is the same Jacob who once stole his father Isaac's blessing from his older brother, Esau. One of the most poignant moments in Genesis (27:38) is Esau's cry to his father:

"Have you but one blessing, my father? Bless me, even me also… And Esau lifted up his voice and wept."

Not one of us ever outgrows our need for blessings!

Adapted from *Your Legacy Matters*

Appendix VI: Your First Covid Legacy Letter

My hope is that you will find deep satisfaction as your needs are met through legacy writing. These needs, often unspoken, include: to belong, to be known, to be remembered, to make a difference, to bless and be blessed, to put your life in order, to deepen your sense of self, and to celebrate life.

> "The ethical will [legacy letter] is a wonderful gift
> to leave to your family at the end of your life,
> but I think its main importance is
> what it gives you in the midst of life."
>
> — Andrew Weil, M.D.

Start with Purpose

Before writing, set an intention. Below is the purpose statement I included in *Your Legacy Matters*. You are welcome to adapt it as you wish for your own COVID legacy letter:

> "I believe it both a privilege and a responsibility to record, communicate and preserve family and community histories and values, document the legacies we've

> received, and the experiences we've lived that make each of us who we uniquely are. Preserving our wisdom and love establishes a link in the chain of generations and passes on a legacy for those of tomorrow's world. Legacy writing is one of the ways we can fulfill our individual and communal covenant with the past and the future."

Robert Baden-Powell offers timeless wisdom about the legacy we leave:

"No one can pass through life,
any more than he can pass through a bit of country,
without leaving tracks behind,
and those tracks may often be helpful
to those coming after him in finding their way."

Prepare Your Writing Space

Once your purpose is clear, gather your materials: a journal, blank paper, your favorite pen or pencil, an eraser, and a timer. If possible, create a calm and beautiful space dedicated to your writing. Settle into your chair with a cup of tea or coffee, and if you choose you may light a candle or place a meaningful object nearby.

If you write digitally, make your setup equally intentional and comforting.

Begin with Reflection:

Open your journal and read any entries from the Covid years. If you kept notes in this book, review them as well. Choose one meaningful moment, experience, or lesson learned to explore. Set your timer for 20—30 minutes. and begin writing the **context** of your letter—followed by the **story** you've selected.

When the timer rings, pause. You can return later to reread what you wrote, edit as needed, and begin the next part: your **learning** from the experience – a value, some wisdom, a surprise that you didn't see before you began to write – and voila! Your third paragraph is written.

Finally, compose your **blessing,** words that flow naturally from your story and reflection. If you're unsure how to craft this, revisit the blessing in my sample letter or those shared by other writers in the book.

Congratulations! You've completed your first COVID–19 legacy letter.

What Comes Next?

Before writing another, return to your journal and reflect on this first experience. What did it reveal about you? What surprised you? Consider whether you want to write more letters using the writing exercise, prompts, or readings in this book as inspiration.

All of us have been sorely tested over the past five years. While grief and loss continue, so too does resilience – if we choose to see it. As Pauline Boss reminds us: recognizing the effects of COVID-19 can strengthen our resilience, allowing healing to begin for ourselves, our families, our communities, and the world.

My blessing to Legacy Writers

May your personal experiences expand the growing body of knowledge about COVID-19. May your words offer healing and resilience to others still experiencing this yet unfinished global pandemic.

May you and your legacy letters be blessed – with tears and joy, honesty and compassion, peace in your losses, and hope and resilience for yourself, your loved ones, and future generations.

Appendix VII: A Curated List for Readers: Recommended COVID Fiction

If you're interested in exploring some of the most powerful fiction written during and about the pandemic, from its onset in 2020 through today, you'll find a curated list below. These books span genres and perspectives. Enjoy!

Blindness by Jose Saramago; Mariner Books, 2013. "Hit by an epidemic of 'white blindness', the population succumbs to fear and desperation."

Hello Beautiful by Ann Napolitano; The Dial Press, 2023. Grief is rendered with deep tenderness in this novel: "Articulating grief in a way I needed to heal after losing my dad and uncle to Covid in the pandemic."

The Glass Maker by Tracy Chevalier, Viking, 2024. Follows glass- making women in Murano, Italy. The Renaissance-era plague there mirrors COVID, when infected families were locked inside and the sick removed to isolated islands outside Venice. The final chapter brings us to the present catastrophe.

The Rich People Have Gone Away: a Novel by Regina Porter; Hogarth, 2024. A brilliant social commentary: "She uses the COVID pandemic… as a prism to separate the mingled wavelengths of American society. The virus itself may not have discriminated, but it was endured by different kinds of people in tragically different ways." She's equally interested in the way Covid interacted with an older and more pernicious virus, racism.

The Vulnerables by Sigrid Nunez; Riverhead Press, 2023. A striking insight from page 12: "Perhaps what is wanted in our own dark, anti-truth times, with all our blatant hypocrisy and the growing use of story as a means to distort and obscure reality, is a literature of personal history and reflection: direct, authentic, scrupulous about fact."

Wish You Were Here by Jodi Picoult, Ballantine Books, 2021. A carefully planned life is upended by the pandemic: "That was how I learned that the world changes between heartbeats; that life is never an absolute, but always a wager."

Year of Wonders by Geraldine Brooks, Penguin Books, 2002. Set in a 1666 English village ravished by plague, the protagonist grapples with the spiritual, physical, and emotional devastation of a collapsing community.

Thrillers set during lockdown: Each suspenseful tale captures the eerie atmosphere of pandemic isolation and restricted movement.

by Elly Griffiths: *The Locked Room*

by Catherine Ryan Howard: *56 Days*

by Peter May: **Lockdown**

For children:

Diary of a Quarantined Kid by Louis G. Lyu, Lulu Publishing, 2023. Written by an 8-year-old boy whose world is turned upside down by the pandemic; he finds support and hope in family and friends.

"In the Time of the Pandemic" A poem written by Kitty O'Meara that appears at the end of this book's introduction, later published as a picture book of the same title (Tra Publishing, 2020). It presents her message to children aged 4-8.

Acknowledgements

Writing this book has been a sacred journey for me. Using all my legacy writing skills to approach one of the most significant and deadly events of our time was more than a challenge; it tested everything I knew, everything I didn't know, and asked me to open fully to my own spiritual nature, to humility, and to help from Above.

For the legacy and psychological knowledge, wisdom and encouragement I received, I am deeply grateful to Pauline Boss, PhD, Susan Griffin, and Rabbis Joseph Edelheit and Larry Raphael.

I would be remiss if I didn't credit my devoted senior legacy facilitator team: Judith Breier, Bill Marsella, Susanna Schuerman, and Michael Ziomko for their personal contributions to this book and to our work together planting legacy deeper into the world. (See Life-Legacies.com)

Words fail to express my appreciation for the support I've received from friends, readers of early and later drafts, and Susie Kaufman's crucial recommendation to strengthen my voice. I am so grateful to Teresa Schreiber Werth and Dan Taylor for their thoughtful reading of my final draft and their gracious and brilliant writing of the Preface and Forward.

Special thanks to my granddaughter Gigi, who brought my dream cover to fruition; she also introduced me to Clara, my AI editor from ChatGPT. Clara offered unwavering respect for the heart of this book. She helped me tighten my often-rambling sentences. Thanks also to Clara for assisting me in choosing fonts and formatting to complement the content of the book.

It was my special privilege for my grandson, Isaac Joseph Julson, to conceive with his full heart, creative mind, and talented paintbrush the powerful frontispiece gracing this book.

Most of all I am indebted to those who unselfishly and generously gifted a community of strangers with their writing to support their healing (and ours). See their names in the Contributors section below.

Contributors:

Martha Albrecht

Angelina Aller

Minx Boren

Judith Breier

Joan Connor

Sarah Bourne Crosby

Ronnie Dunetz

Carol Ferris

Katrina Freese

Julie Gardner

Patsy Glista

Kathi Gowsell

Anne K. Gross

Dustin Gross

Laura Hammond

A. Stuart Hanson

Ann Haas

Isaac Joseph Julson

Susie Kaiufman

Elliot Kirschner

Bill Marsella

Maureen Mitchell

Mary Myers

Jeri Okamoto-Tanaka

Kitty O'Meara

James Parker

Michelle Riddell

Susanna Schuerman

Linda N. Spencer

Gigi Stillman

Paloma Sullkin

Daniel Taylor

Margaret (Peggy) Thompson

Susan Tilsch

Joanne Turnbull

Lynn Unger

Carol Weinstock

Teresa Schreiber Werth

Karen West

Michael Ziomko

Bibliography

Albrecht, Martha. Reflection. n.d.

Albom, Mitch. *Tuesdays With Morrie.* New York: Doubleday, 1997.

Altman, Millys. *Year of the Flu: A World War I Medical Thriller.* Kindle Scribe, 2017.

Anversa, David. *History of Pandemics.* Independently Published, 2020.

———. *The 1918 Spanish Influenza Pandemic.* Independently Published, 2020.

Arnold, Catharine. *Pandemic 1918: Eyewitness Accounts from the Greatest Medical Holocaust in Modern History.* New York: St. Martin's Griffin, 2020.

Atwood, Margaret. *Oryx and Crake.* New York: Anchor Books, 2003.

Boren, Minx. *Untitled poems.* 2021.

Boss, Pauline. *Ambiguous Loss: Learning to Live with Unresolved Grief.* Cambridge, MA: Harvard University Press, 2000.

———. *The Myth of Closure: Ambiguous Loss in a Time of Pandemic and Change.* New York: W.W. Norton, 2022.

Brener, Anne. *Mourning and Mitzvah.* Woodstock, VT: Jewish Lights Publishing, 1993.

Breier, Judith. *Legacy Letter.* n.d.

Brooks, Geraldine. *Year of Wonders.* New York: Penguin Books, 2002.

Chevalier, Tracy. *The Glass Maker.* New York: Viking, 2024.

Collier, Richard. *The Plague of the Spanish Lady.* London: Allison & Busby, 1996.

Cook, Robin. *Pandemic.* New York: G.P. Putnam's Sons, 2019.

Cornish, David. *1918: The Great Pandemic.* David Cornish, 2013.

Crosby, Sarah Bourns. *"We've All Been Exposed." Poem* n.d. *https://sarahbournscrosby.com*

Dunetz, Ronnie. *"Reflections of Children of Holocaust Survivors in Their Second Half of Life on Their Life Experiences."* Unpublished dissertation, The Wisdom School at Ubiquity University, 2023.

Emerson, Ralph Waldo. *Quote.* n.d.

Faulkner, William. *Quote. Requiem for a Nun.* New York: Random House, 1951.

Ferris, Carol. *Reflection. n.d.*

StacFelson, Irit, and Amit Shrira. *"Parental PTSD and Psychological Reactions during the COVID-19 Pandemic among Offspring of Holocaust Survivors." Psychological Trauma: Theory, Research, Practice, and Policy. Yeshiva University News, 2021.*

Frankl, Viktor. *Quote. n.d.*

Freed, Rachael. *Your Legacy Matters. Minneapolis: MinervaPress, 2013.*

Fritz, Charles. *"The Legacy of Building Community." In Tribe by Sebastian Junger, New York: Twelve, 2016.*

Garrett, Laurie. *The Coming Plague. n.d.*

Gawande, Atul. *"The Aftermath of a Pandemic Requires as Much Focus as the Start." The New York Times, March 16, 2023.*

Glista, Patsy. *Grief poems. n.d.*

Gorman, Amanda. *"Pre-Memory." Quote. n.d.*

Griffin, Susan. *A Chorus of Stones: The Private Life of War. New York: Doubleday, 1992.*

Gross, Anne K. *The Polio Journals: Lessons from My Mother. Diversity Press, 2011.*

Gross, Justin. *Forbidden History: Volume 3: Plagues, Prophets, and People Who Should Not Have Been in Charge. Kindle, 2025.*

Hadfield, Robert John. *Virus 1918. n.d.*

Hammonds, Laura. *"Shots and Stuff." Unpublished poem, 2021.*

Hanson, A. Stuart. *A Senior's Guide for Living Well and Dying Well. Wolfe Lake Press, 2022.*

Hemingway, Ernest. *Quote. n.d.*

Julson, Isaac Joseph. *Artist's Painting. n.d.*

Kaufman, Susie. *Reflection. n.d.*

Kierkegaard, Søren. *Quote. n.d.*

LeBor, Adam. *City of Oranges: An Intimate History of Arabs and Jews in Jaffa. New York: W.W. Norton, 2007.*

Lewis, Michael. *The Premonition. New York: W.W. Norton, 2021.*

Lindsay, Stacey. *"Interview with Anna Quindlen." Maria Shriver's Sunday Paper, April 29, 2022. https://www.annaquindlen.net.*

Lovecraft, H.P. *"The Rats in the Walls." Weird Tales Magazine, March 1924.*

Nachman, *Rabbi of Bratslav (1772-1810). Prayer. n.d.*

Napolitano, Ann. *Hello Beautiful. New York: Dial Press, 2023.*

NPR. *"Book Review by Jeevika Verma: Call Us What We Carry by Amanda Gorman." December 6, 2021.*

O'Meara, Kitty. *In the Time of the Pandemic. Tra Publishers, 2020.*

Palmer, Parker. *Quote. n.d.*

Parker, James. *"Corona Prayer." The Atlantic, April 19, 2020.*

Parker-Post, *Tara. "Parents Pack." The Washington Post, March 16, 2023.https://www.chop.edu/news/feature-article-flashback-parenting-and-summer-1950s.*

Perrin, Valerie. *Fresh Water for Flowers. New York: Europa Editions, 2020.*

Picoult, Jodi. *Wish You Were Here. New York: Random House, 2022.*

Plouffe, David. *A Citizen's Guide to Beating Donald Trump. New York: Viking, 2020.*

Pogrebin, Abigail, and Rabbi Dov Liner. *It Takes Two to Torah. New York: Fig Tree Books, 2024.*

Riddell, Michelle. *"You Will Want to Remember This." Poem. Facebook, n.d.*

Rilke, Rainer Maria. *Quote. n.d.*

Rosen, Rutha. *Poem n.d.(circa 2020)*

Roth, Philip. *Nemesis. New York: Vintage, 2011.*

Roy, Arundhati. *"The Pandemic is a Portal. "YES! Magazine. April 17, 2020.*

Saramago, José. *Blindness. Boston: Mariner Books, 1999.*

Shaer, Matthew. *"Why Is the Loneliness Epidemic So Hard to 'Cure'?" New York Times Magazine, August 27, 2024.*

Shelley, Mary Wollstonecraft. *The Last Man. Ware, UK: Wordsworth Editions, 2004.*

Sima, Richard and George Wylesol. *"The Science of Forgetting: Why We're Already Losing Pandemic Memories." Washington Post, March 13, 2023.*

Smokler, Erin Leib. *Torah in a Time of Plague. Ben Yehuda Press, 2021.*

Soloveichik, Meir. *"Parashah and Politics: How Torah Changed the World." Tikvah, November 5, 2024.*

Spencer, Linda N. *"The Color of Stillness." Reflection. n.d.*

Spinney, Laura. *Pale Rider: The Spanish Flu of 1918 and How It Changed the World. New York: PublicAffairs, 2018.*

Spiro, James. *"How StartUp Nation and the IDF Support Each Other." Michael Oren's Substack, August 1, 2024.*

St. John Mandel, Emily. *Station Eleven. New York: Vintage Books, 2014.*

Stulberg, Brad. *Master of Change. New York: Harper One, 2023.*

Taylor, Daniel. *Creating a Spiritual Legacy. Ada, Michigan. Brazos Press, 2011.*

Thurber, James. *Quote. n.d.*

Tillich, Susan Eastman. *Reflection. n.d.*

Tolstoy, Leo. *Quote. n.d.*

Ungar, Lynn. *"Pandemic." Poem. n.d.*

Vonnegut, Kurt. *Slaughterhouse-Five. New York: Dial Press, 1999.*

Wallace-Wells, *David. "Covid: Why Is It a Surprise That America Is Gloomy After a Devastating Pandemic?" New York Times, December 6, 2023.*

Weil, Andrew. *Quote. n.d.*

Weinstock, Carol. *Two humorous poems. n.d.*

Weller, Francis. *The Wild Edge of Sorrow. Berkeley: North Atlantic Books, 2015.*

Werth, Adam A. *Artist's illustration. n.d.*

Werth, Teresa Schreiber. *Navigating the Pandemic: Stories of Hope and Resilience. New York: Page Publishing, 2021.*

Westheimer, Ruth. *The Joy of Connections. New York: Rodale Books, 2024.*

Wheatley, Margaret. *Quote about loneliness. n.d.*

Wiesel, Elie. *Quotes about Story and Memory. n.d.*

Wright, Lawrence. *"The Plague Year." The New Yorker, December 28, 2020.*

Ziomko, Michael. *Letter to daughter. Reflections on potting and community. n.d.*

Index

A

B

C

D

E

F

G

H

I

J

K

L

M

N

O

P

Q

R

S

V

W

Y

Z

About the Author

Rachael Freed, MSW, LICSW, is a nationally recognized pioneer in the legacy-writing movement and a senior fellow at the University of Minnesota's Earl E. Bakken Center for Spirituality & Healing. Her work centers on legacy writing—adapted from the ancient tradition of the ethical will—as a powerful tool for reflection, healing, and intergenerational connection.

Freed is the author of *Your Legacy Matters, Women's Lives, Women's Legacies: Passing Your Beliefs and Blessings to Future Generations, and The Legacy Workbook for the Busy Woman*. Her book *Life and Loss: Legacy Writing in the Age of COVID-19,* published in 2026, reflects what she considers her most significant contribution, advocating legacy writing as a meaningful response to collective grief, disruption, and change.

She is the founder of **Life-Legacies**, a mission-driven project dedicated to making legacy writing accessible and meaningful for people of all ages. Over the years, she has trained more than fifty facilitators and guided thousands of participants worldwide through workshops, courses, and writing groups. Her writing appears regularly on Substack, and her work has been featured in national publications and interfaith communities.

Freed has facilitated legacy writing programs at diverse venues, including AARP–New York, the Commonwealth Club of San Francisco, Sage-ing International, and the U.S. Holocaust Museum in Washington, D.C. Known for blending social history, spirituality, and personal reflection, she brings warmth, depth, and clarity to conversations about loss, resilience, and remembrance.

Her volunteer work includes two years with the U.S. Peace Corps in Tunisia, more than twenty years reading for the Minnesota

Society for the Blind, and leadership in adult education and community legacy initiatives at Temple Israel in Minneapolis.

Earlier in her career, Freed counseled cardiac families for over twenty years and trained cardiac professionals internationally. She is the author *of Heartmates: A Guide for the Spouse and Family of the Heart Patient* and *The Heartmates Journal,* the only resources devoted to the emotional and spiritual recovery of families living with heart disease.